JENNY'S STORY

I almost stopped breathing. I felt something coming from my stomach up to my chest, like choking. I started talking and my voice sounded funny to me—like it was someone else's. I hoped I didn't sound that scared to him.

"Look, I didn't know you had this in mind. Honestly. Maybe you thought I did, but I didn't. Please take me home."

"I will."

He said it as if he was being very calm and reasonable, but he didn't move.

"Now. Come on."

Then he reached into the pocket of his jacket and took something out—I couldn't see what it was. He started turning it over in his hand.

He said, "You seemed like a nice kid before. Back there, before—when we were talking. But now I don't know."

Then I saw he had a pocketknife. He saw I was staring at it.

"You know what this is? Don't worry—I'm not even going to open it."

He tossed it on the dashboard—it slid across and stopped against the windshield. I grabbed the door handle and tried to get out of the car, but he caught me by the arm and I couldn't get away.

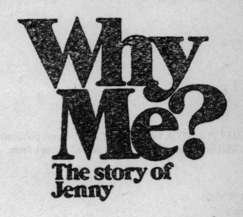

Why Me?

The story of Jenny

PATRICIA DIZENZO

AN AVON FLARE BOOK

WHY ME? THE STORY OF JENNY is an original publication of Avon
Books. This work has never before appeared in book form.

AVON BOOKS
A division of
The Hearst Corporation
105 Madison Avenue
New York, New York 10016

Copyright © 1976 by Patricia Dizenzo
Published by arrangement with the author
Library of Congress Catalog Card Number: 76-1489
ISBN: 0-380-00563-8

First Avon Books Printing: March 1976
First Avon Flare Printing: January 1982

AVON FLARE BOOKS TRADEMARK REG. U.S. PAT. OFF. AND IN OTHER
COUNTRIES, MARCA REGISTRADA, HECHO EN U.S.A.

Printed in Canada

UNV   28 27 26 25 24 23 22 21

I stayed home from school again. I'll go tomorrow. I have to. Mother gave me a funny look last night—she knows something's wrong, at least she's wondering. Another day and she'll give me a hard time, and maybe tell Daddy. I'll go crazy if they both start in on me.

I know I've got to see a doctor. I don't want to go to Dr. Garrett. Doctors are supposed to respect their patient's privacy, but I know he'd go ahead and use his own judgment—which means he'd tell them, no matter what I said.

There's a bruise on my leg—I didn't see it before.

❀ ❀ ❀

Missed another day of school. I didn't mean to—just couldn't get myself together. I set the alarm for seven so I'd have plenty of time, got up, dressed, fixed my hair, but when it was time to go I couldn't. I suddenly felt like I couldn't handle it—classes, teachers, seeing people all day. My stomach felt funny and my hands were all clammy. I got undressed and went back to bed and tried to calm down. When Mother came into my room I told her I was still sick. I guess she believed me.

I couldn't sleep. After she left for work I went down to the living room and turned on the television. I sat around and watched game shows and soap operas all day, didn't even get dressed. I tried to do some History but I couldn't concentrate. I practically started crying I felt so frustrated, like something is really wrong with me.

Mother came home early and caught me in the kitchen. I was making something to take up to my room so I wouldn't have to eat with them. She said I ought to go and see a doctor about my virus. She wanted to take my temperature—I told her I'd already taken it and it was about a hundred. I could tell she didn't believe me, but she didn't say anything. She started talking about school, how I shouldn't be missing days senior year, how I had to keep up my grades if I wanted to get into college. I was making tea and laying things on a tray, trying to keep my hands steady. She had to throw Robby's marks up at me—my perfect brother. I was so nervous I dropped a plate. I could feel her watching me while I picked up the pieces. She asked me if I really had a virus—she said she wanted to know what was going on. I got upset—I said she was crazy, why didn't she ever believe me? I didn't mean to have an argument with her but she was getting me so upset. She wouldn't leave me alone. I went upstairs. She didn't follow me and she didn't call me to dinner. I don't know what she told Dad.

I started thinking about my period again, hoping it'll come on time.

I looked into the mirror trying to see what I looked like—what I'd look like to someone else. I didn't see any difference. I have those little circles under my eyes from not sleeping—I've had them before. I look the same.

I have to wash my hair for school.

Last Sunday I didn't want to stay home. I was just sitting around thinking about Monday and the weekend being over. Mother and Dad were going over to Uncle Jerry's and I didn't want to go. I didn't want to see Laura for one thing—all she ever talks about is her new clothes and how she lost more weight. I called Clara to see what she was doing and asked her if she wanted to come over. She said she'd meet me for a coke at Lenny's, which is about halfway between our houses. I had left my chemistry book in my locker Friday and I needed it so she said she'd bring hers. I also wanted to talk to her about her party. I was thinking of asking John Fenton and I wanted to ask her if she knew if Sonia was planning to ask him. My parents knew I was going out. I left a little after they did.

It was very cold out, more like winter than fall. About halfway to Lenny's I wished I'd put on a scarf and gloves, but it was too far to go back. I had on a thin jacket and the wind was going right through me.

When I saw the neon sign in Lenny's parking lot I almost started running.

The place was almost empty. It looked completely different from Saturday nights when everyone from the high school is there. There were just a few people sitting at the counter, no one in the booths. Eddie Farrell was working at the counter. I knew him from the summer—we had worked together, waiting on tables. I was surprised to see Eddie. I didn't know he worked all year round—I had never been to Lenny's on a Sunday night before. We started talking and he made me a hot chocolate. He hadn't seen Clara. I asked him if he thought Barini would give me my job back for the summer. He said he'd ask for me.

He had to wait on a customer so I went over to the booths in front where I could see Clara when she came in. I sat there drinking my hot chocolate, trying to warm up, watching the traffic go by on the highway. It was already dark out. I waited about twenty minutes and Clara still hadn't showed up. She had said she was going to leave her house at six, the same time as me, so I didn't know what had happened.

Finally I went to the pay phone in back and called her house. She answered. She said her parents had gone out at the last minute and she had to stay home with her little brother. It was too cold and late for her to take him out. She had called my house, but it must have been right after I left. I was mad because I'd come all that way for nothing and she hadn't even bothered to call Lenny's and say she wasn't going to be there. Someone would have taken the message and told me. We had an argument over the phone. She said I could come on over to her house, but I didn't want to—it was too far to walk in that weather and besides I was annoyed.

I went back to the booth and sat there trying to

make up my mind to leave. I was looking out the window when someone behind me said, "It's going to snow." I looked around and saw a boy, about nineteen, standing near the booth. I had seen him at the counter when I came in—he had on a red-and-black plaid jacket. He was looking out the front windows at the highway. I didn't think he was talking to me, but there was no one else around. I didn't say anything—just kept looking out the window at the parking lot in front. Then he said, "Are you waiting for someone?"

I was surprised he was still there. I told him I had been waiting for someone.

"Me too. It seems like I'm always waiting for someone."

I said, "Maybe you picked the wrong place."

He smiled like it was quite funny and sat down in the booth across from me. It was the first time I really looked at him closely. I thought he was eighteen or nineteen—a couple of years older than me anyway. He had straight blond hair, fairly long. He seemed okay, but I wasn't in a mood to talk to anyone. I looked out the window again. I was about to leave.

He started drumming his fingers on the table.

"Maybe. Maybe I picked the wrong place. Maybe."

That was all he said. He made me a little nervous, but I was always that way with boys if I couldn't think of anything to say. I didn't think anything of it.

Finally he asked me, "Are you from around here?"

"Yeah—I go to the high school. How about you?"

"I'm in college."

"Oh, yeah? Where?"

"Community College, Morrisville. I live at home—here in town. I'm a commuter—a day student."

I asked him if he had gone to the high school. He said he had. We started talking about teachers. I asked him who he'd had senior year.

9

He said, "I had all of them." He gave me a look as if it was a bad memory.

"Did you have Miller for history?"

"Oh yeah—I had Miller."

"Did you like her?"

"She was okay."

"Did you take Italian?"

"No."

"What language?"

"Spanish."

"Oh, you had Montesinos."

"Yeah."

"How about Corry? Did you take chemistry?"

"I sure did take chemistry."

I started laughing—the way he said it.

"I get the feeling you didn't like high school."

He said, "College is better. There's more freedom."

"That's what I hear."

"Even if you live at home. I commute."

"Yeah, you said. I might do that—my parents don't want me to go far."

He started staring at the top of the table as if he didn't know what to say next. He was tracing figure eights with his finger, and then some other kind of pattern. Just to say something I asked him what he was majoring in.

"I haven't decided. Engineering maybe. If you want to know the truth I'm—I'm in it more for the social life."

Something about the way he said "social life" gave me a funny feeling. I couldn't imagine him having a lot of friends and "socializing" a lot. I thought he was shy but trying to pretend he wasn't. That's the feeling I got from talking to him. But it didn't take him long to start up a conversation with me, and I wasn't even encouraging him at first, so maybe I was wrong.

I finally decided to go. I got out of the booth and put on my jacket.

He said, "I'm going too."

He walked out the door and held it open for me—then we stood around in the parking lot in front. He offered to give me a lift home. I told him no, I lived close by. I was trying to figure out what to do. I had never gone out with a boy in college before, but I could tell he was thinking about asking me out and then I started thinking about asking him to Clara's party. It was cold standing outside. I was trying to keep my back to the wind, trying to keep warm. I didn't want to leave and I didn't want to stay either—I didn't know what to do.

"You won't take a ride from me, huh?"

"Right."

"What's your phone number? Maybe I could call you sometime."

"Okay."

I wrote my number on a piece of paper I had in my pocket, also my name—he didn't even know it, and I didn't know his. I started to ask him but I didn't—I thought it would just come up naturally. He took the paper and put it in his jacket.

"You'll give me your phone number, but you won't take a ride from me, right?"

"Right."

"Where's the logic in that?"

"I don't know."

He looked as cold as I was. His jacket wasn't that heavy and he didn't have gloves either. I could see his breath frosting in the cold air, my own too.

I asked him where his car was—there were only three in the parking lot. Saturday nights it was full. He pointed to an old blue Chevy parked around the side of the building.

"It's not mine. My car's in the garage. This belongs to a friend of mine.

"Oh, sure. You've got a new Jaguar getting repaired, right?"

I only meant to kid him but I was sorry I said it. He looked embarrassed, like I'd humiliated him—as if I was making fun of him for not having much money. I didn't mean that but it must have sounded that way. I started talking nervously, saying anything, trying to change the subject and smooth it over—I was saying I didn't have a car, I didn't even have my license yet. I told him how Robby was supposed to teach me this year when he came home for vacations because I didn't want my parents to do it. I told him how I was afraid of Dad being too strict and Mother being too nervous—I didn't think either one of them would have any confidence in me as a driver. I was trying to make him laugh, but he still seemed to be thinking about something else. I decided to take the ride—I asked him if he was sure it wasn't out of his way.

He said, "No. Come on—it's cold."

I got into the car. It wasn't any warmer, but at least there was no wind. He got in and started the ignition. He smiled at me and said, "Girls don't have to learn to drive. They don't need cars."

"Are you kidding? I could use one."

I didn't think anything of what he said. He turned on the heater—he said it would take a few minutes to warm up. I thought he was still apologizing for the car so I said I was warm enough. There was some warm air coming in. I could feel it on my legs.

"Where do you live?"

"Temple Street. Off Central Avenue."

"Oh, yeah. I know where it is." He started the car. "You have an older brother?"

"Yeah—four years older. He's going to graduate from college next year."

"Same as me."

"What are you—nineteen?"

"Twenty."

He was looking ahead, concentrating on driving and not looking at me. He turned into the highway and crossed over to the southbound lane. I told him to take the turnoff to Temple about a quarter of a mile down the road. I was thinking about Clara's party and trying to figure out if any older kids would be there. She had a cousin in college who came to her last one and brought a friend. I didn't want to ask a college boy and then have him come and be disgusted because everyone was too young. I was going to say something about the party, but then he missed the turnoff.

I said, "You'll have to go down to the traffic circle now. I don't know how you're going to turn around here."

"It's Temple Street?"

"Yes, but you have to get onto Central."

"I know how to get there."

He drove a little further, but before he reached the traffic circle he took a turnoff past a closed filling station. The road led into the part of town where all the factories were. There were no houses or stores so it was deserted Sundays. There were a lot of low factory buildings along the roads and further off I could see a row of trucks parked near some warehouses. The buildings were all closed. There were a few streetlights along the road on the corners—they were the only lights. I didn't like the way it looked.

I said to him, "You're better off going down to the traffic circle like I said. I don't know where this road leads."

13

"I know how to get to Temple from here."

He was looking ahead at the streets as if he had to concentrate so he wouldn't get lost. None of the streets were marked with signs that I could see. Then he said, "I have to double back."

I didn't say anything. I was afraid he wanted to park somewhere and I'd be in for an argument. He drove two more blocks, then he turned into a driveway that led behind a brick building. He stopped the car there and sat staring at the steering wheel, not looking at me.

I said, "Okay. You can take me home now."

He didn't move or even turn his head to look at me. He said, "I'm not from this town."

I froze even though I wasn't sure what it meant. I tried not to let anything show in my voice.

"No? Where are you from?"

"Out of state."

"Okay, you fooled me. Take me home."

I moved away on the seat—I turned so I could look straight at him. My back was against the door. He was still staring ahead.

He said, "I'd better tell you something right now. I didn't like your tone of voice just then."

I thought of getting out of the car and walking back to the highway, but I figured it would be worse for him to see I was scared. He kept talking—it was like he was talking to himself.

"Disguises. That's the name of the game."

I didn't think I heard him right.

"What?"

"You say you want a car. I don't see that. Some girls want to have everything their own way."

He turned to me and that was the first time he looked straight at me since we got in the car. He said, "That's the truth, isn't it?"

14

I didn't know what to say. I didn't know what he was talking about.

He said, "You're pretty full of yourself, aren't you?"

"Look, I want to go home now."

"If there's anything that gets me it's a girl like you. You think you can do anything you want, just snap your fingers."

I started to say I wasn't like that but I couldn't. He kept talking.

"You're supposed to be the gentle sex. You know that, don't you? You're well on your way. And they get away with it. I bought it. No one can mess you up like a woman. What are you, a woman or a girl?"

I didn't answer him.

"No one can lie like a woman. They get away with it—just as long as they have their pretty faces and can swing their little tails around. But I don't like to hurt anyone—especially girls."

I almost stopped breathing. I felt something coming from my stomach up to my chest, like a fist. I started talking and my voice sounded funny to me—like it was someone else's. I was hoping I didn't sound that scared.

"Look, I didn't know you had this in mind. Honestly. Maybe you thought I did, but I didn't. Please take me home."

"I will."

He said it as if he was being very calm and reasonable, but he didn't move.

"Now. Come on."

Then he reached into the pocket of his jacket and took something out—I couldn't see what it was. He started turning it over in his hand.

He said, "You seemed like a nice kid before. Back there, before—when we were talking. But now I don't know."

Then I saw he had a pocketknife. He saw me staring at it.

"You know what this is? Don't worry—I'm not even going to open it."

He tossed it on the dashboard. It slid across and stopped against the windshield. I grabbed the door handle and tried to get out of the car, but he caught me by the arm and I couldn't get away.

"Don't try that. I warned you."

"Please—"

"I warned you about that. I don't like—Don't get me mad."

"I haven't done anything to you. Please. Let me go."

I was looking away from him at the dashboard and it started to look fuzzy—I was afraid I was going to faint. I didn't scream or start crying. I had the feeling that it would make it worse if I lost control of myself.

He said, "Don't act so innocent. I hate that. You know why you came here and I know it."

I didn't try to pull away from him then. I could feel the grip he had on my arm through my jacket and he was too strong. I was afraid of getting him mad. I didn't know what he'd do. He pushed down the lock on the door on my side, then he opened the door on his side and got out and pulled me out after him. Once I was standing I tried to get away, but I couldn't. He said he'd kill me if I tried it again. There was so much hatred in his eyes, as if he had known me for a long time and had always hated me, and now he was getting even. He made me get into the back seat and take off some of my clothes. Then he raped me. I didn't scream or cry. I almost felt like it was happening to someone else. I was scared of what he was going to do after. I was trying to think what I should do. I didn't get all hysterical and out of control. He was calling me some filthy names; I just kept trying to talk to myself—not out loud, but keeping some words in my mind so I wouldn't hear what he said.

When he was through he let me go and sat up. I started putting on my things, not looking at him, hoping he wouldn't try to stop me. I was trying to keep my hands from shaking—I could hardly get dressed. He noticed I started crying a little.

He said, "What are you crying about? It doesn't matter. You're garbage."

I didn't look at him but I could tell from his voice he was different, laughing at me, not so angry anymore.

I got out of the car. He didn't try to stop me. I started walking back to the highway and, when I got a little way from the car, I started running, I was afraid he was going to change his mind and come after me but he didn't. When I was almost up to the highway I looked back. The car was still there. Then the red taillights came on and the car started out of the driveway and turned in the other direction, away from the highway. It passed under a streetlight and I realized I hadn't looked at the license plate. I wasn't thinking about anything like that.

There weren't any sidewalks on the part of the highway past the bridge and I had a hard time walking. There was a lot of traffic—I was glad, it made me feel safer. The wind was as cold as before. I ran part of the way. It took me almost an hour to get to my house.

My parents were home. I could see the lights on in the living room and I could hear the television. I didn't know what I looked like. I went in by the back door and went straight up the stairs and locked myself in the bathroom.

When I was there the warmth of the house came

17

over me all of a sudden. I didn't realize how cold it was out. I thought I was going to throw up. I went to the sink and stood there, but the feeling went away—I wasn't sick. I started taking off my clothes. There was blood on my underpants and it had soaked through to my slacks too. I started washing them in cold water in the sink. I kept thinking, I'm safe now.

I took a shower and washed my hair. When I was done I opened the door and listened. I heard my parents talking—they were both downstairs. I went into my room and put on my pajamas. I didn't know if I was going to keep on bleeding. I got a Kotex. I put my clothes on the radiator in my room so they'd dry overnight and Mother wouldn't see them wet and wonder why I had washed them. All this time I was feeling very strange, doing everything very calmly, like a machine. There were only a few things to do and then everything was clean.

I turned out the light in my room so they'd think I was asleep and not come in. When I was in bed I started trembling. I pulled the blankets around me and that stopped it. I could hardly believe I was back in my bed, and the room was so quiet and peaceful—everything exactly the same way it always was. I kept thinking, I might have been killed.

I didn't understand what had happened—I knew but I couldn't really understand it in some way. I didn't know why I had gotten into the car with him, why I hadn't been able to tell. I could hardly think about it. In one way I was upset, in another I was relieved. I couldn't believe it had happened and I couldn't believe it was over. I started crying but I was afraid my parents would hear something so I stopped.

That was three days ago, Sunday.

* * *

Clara came over with my books. She had gotten my History and English assignments from Miller and Schultz. She stayed a little while—we sat in my room and she told me what was going on in school. She was still planning her party. I could tell she didn't notice anything different about me. I thought of asking her if she knew a doctor I could go to, but I couldn't bring it up with her. I would have had to tell her why and I couldn't. It was because of the kind of person she is—she's too smart to have done what I did and she would never understand how I got into a situation like that.

I told her I might go in Friday. She said I should try so I could go over to Marlene Gordon's Friday night and not be stuck at home all weekend.

I felt better when Clara left. Listening to her talk calmed me down a little after my fight with Mother about my "virus."

About ten o'clock Dad knocked on my door and said he wanted to talk to me. I felt very tense when I heard his voice—I didn't know what she had told him. He wasn't in a bad mood—he just asked me how I was and if I thought they should call the doctor. I told him the same thing I told Mother. I said the fight was partly my fault but she got me mad picking on me when I was sick. He didn't say anything. He started talking about Rob, who had written a letter saying he might come home before Thanksgiving, and then he began talking about business. He said it was better. He rented the house on Piedmont Street—the lease had been signed. Then he asked me if I had a lot of tests this week. I knew what he was thinking—I was staying home because I had tests I hadn't studied for. He said I'd missed three days already and it was important for me to keep up my grades senior year, because I'd be applying to colleges soon and it would make a big difference. He said if I could get a scholarship it would help a lot. He had a strict attitude about college—he didn't believe in going for the social life. The way he was talking got me nervous. I could tell he was warning me to shape up and he knew it and I knew it, even though he didn't come out and accuse me of anything. I knew I had to go back to school. I told him I would.

Before he left he put his hand on my head as if I had a fever and kissed me on my forehead goodnight. I didn't expect it—started crying after he left.

❀ ❀ ❀

I went back to school today. I didn't feel too good in the morning—couldn't eat anything for breakfast. When I got to Second Street I almost turned around and went home. But I thought about Dad—his voice in my head telling me I had to go. I didn't want more trouble at home so I kept going and it was okay. Only a couple of kids in homeroom asked where I was. It wasn't that big a deal to anyone that I had been out with the flu. Everyone had other things to think about besides me. I don't know what I was expecting—as if everyone was going to stare at me.

I saw Sonia Cris after lunch going into English. She was walking with Marilyn O'Connor and Sandy. She said, "Well, she's back—send up the flares." Then she said I was looking great. She meant it to be nasty because I didn't look too good and she wanted to bring attention to it. She's always hated me—ever since I wouldn't kiss her big behind to get into her crowd. I was dreading seeing her. She's my only real enemy at school—usually she doesn't bother me, but I don't like to see her when I feel like this.

I got my chemistry homework from Corry. He said I have to stay after school next week to make up the labs. I was hoping he'd just let me read the experiments. Everything else was okay. No one called on me in class.

I saw Eddie Farrell in English. I was staring at his back and I suddenly realized it was him. It was a shock—I felt like running out of the room for a second. I hadn't thought about him since he got me the hot chocolate Sunday night. He might have seen me leaving Lenny's. I had forgotten we had a class together—we didn't sit close to each other and never talked in there. My mind started wandering—some things about Sunday. I remembered asking him if he had any of my teachers and he said yes. All those lies, so creepy. All the time Miss Schultz was talking and I was trying to keep my mind on what she was saying—I didn't want to think about the other. It was a strange feeling listening to her. I felt like an outsider, as if I didn't really belong there.

I had the feeling all day that my face looked funny—as if it was dirty or something. I knew it wasn't, but I kept going to the girls room between classes and looking in the mirror to check how I looked.

It was a relief to get home—everything seemed to be getting back to normal. It made me realize what a daze I was in before—hanging around the house, crying, doing nothing, feeling afraid of Mother and Dad, watching television like a zombie, feeling afraid of everything. I didn't even know how weird I was acting. I wanted to be alone and hide from everyone but all I did was think a lot of sick thoughts instead of putting it out of my mind. It was the worst thing I could have done.

I still had a couple of hours before Mother came home. I made something to eat. I was thinking about Dad—how I went to school because I was scared of him getting mad. Sometimes I wished he wasn't so strict, but with his voice in my head telling me to do something I could do things I was afraid of or didn't want to do. At least this time it was a good thing—snapped me out of it.

I made an appointment with a doctor. I got his name from the Physicians Advisory Service—I remembered Mother talking about it when she started working for Dr. Grinnell. I just looked it up in the phone book, and the man who answered gave me three names. I asked for gynecologists. One was Peterson, the one Mother goes to, so that was no good, but there's one in Halstead named Iverson. I'll have to take the bus there, but it's just as well he's not one in town. I called his office and the nurse said he didn't have any time for three weeks. I told her it was important—she asked what the problem was. I said I needed an examination. She asked again what the problem was. I said I'd rather talk to the doctor. She let it go at that and gave me an appointment for tomorrow at four. I can get there after school. She didn't ask if I was married or how old I was. I was nervous talking to her. The only thing I was sorry about was that I gave her my real name. I didn't think about that ahead of time and when she asked I froze and couldn't think of a phony name to give her. I wished I hadn't done it but I didn't give her my address or phone number.

After I hung up I thought about the money. I didn't know how much he would charge. I started to call back but then I figured I could ask when I was there. I can't pay tomorrow anyway, I'll have to tell the nurse not to send a bill and give her the wrong address if she asks for it. I can use the money I saved from my summer job. Thank goodness I have it.

I came downstairs for dinner when Dad got home. He talked business—about a white elephant he was trying to sell or rent. He said it was too big for anyone to keep up. The owner thought the state might buy it for an orphanage but the zoning law wouldn't allow it. It's out past Amityville where we almost moved. Mother didn't say anything about our fight and neither did he. They talked about Rob and how he was doing in college. I still hadn't read his letter. I felt better eating at the table as long as I could just listen and eat my meatloaf and not have to say anything.

Then Mother brought up Laura and the subject of how we didn't get along. She said that after all we were cousins and I ought to try to get along with her, at least when the families were getting together for holidays and special occasions. She said I was acting selfish. I said it wasn't my fault for not liking Laura—

23

she was a jerk, very self-centered and selfish. When I went to visit all she ever wanted to do was go up to her room so she could get out all her new clothes including every ugly scarf she ever bought at the five and ten and give me a "fashion show." She didn't even like Grandma—she had made a few snide remarks about her when I was over there Easter. Grandma was old-fashioned, true, but that was because she had been brought up differently. Laura thought she was so superior, but Grandma had twice her brains—not to mention her cooking and all the other things she knew. I told Mother all of that and she couldn't think of anything to say back. Dad didn't say anything.

After dinner I did the dishes, then went up to my room and played some music. Couldn't study. I started thinking about all the things Mother had said at the table—that I was selfish and irresponsible and so forth. It seemed like I won the argument, but then I started thinking how if I had gone with them Sunday it never would have happened.

I played the album of folk songs Robby gave me for my birthday, and started hemming my red skirt. I thought of calling Clara, but I knew I couldn't talk to her about anything on my mind so there was no point. I took a bath and got ready for bed early.

I finally had the nerve to sit down and figure out when my period should come. I didn't mark the last two months on the calendar like I used to, but I remember my last one started in school right before gym and I got an excuse from Miss Elias—so it must have been a Friday, probably September 28. Sunday was October 21. It didn't fall in the middle of my cycle—it wasn't even near the dangerous days. I sort of knew this in the back of my mind, but I was afraid to figure it out in black and white before. I couldn't be pregnant, at least I'm pretty sure. My period should come in a few days.

I'm nervous about seeing the doctor tomorrow. I should have gone Monday instead of putting it off so long and staying in the house worrying. I don't have to tell him the whole story, depending on what he's like. They're used to problems like this. They're just medical problems to them—no reason to feel ashamed.

School was okay Friday. I felt nervous, but not like the first day back. In Italian Miss Farrand called on me to translate—I did ten lines and knew all the vocabulary. That's one class I'm good in even if I never open the book. It made me think of Grandma and I didn't feel so nervous. It was the first time I got called on in class since I got back. I was worrying about it—having to stand up and everyone looking at me. It helped me get my confidence back.

Got an excuse from gym—told Miss Elias I wasn't completely over the flu. I didn't want to wear a gym suit because of my leg. The bruise still showed a little. I got a pass to the study hall in 203, but then I sat there the whole period thinking about the doctor's appointment. It would have been better if I had taken the gym class.

❀ ❀ ❀

After school I walked over to Oldis Street to get the number 73 bus. I thought they ran more often—it didn't come until a quarter of four. When we got to Halstead it was already past four. Dr. Iverson's office was on Pierpont Street. The bus driver didn't know where it was, and he left me off in the middle of town, near the movie theater on Main Street. There were some women waiting at the bus stop and I asked them. One of them knew and she gave me directions. It was about six blocks, not too far. I got there in about ten minutes, walking fast. I was worried all the way since I was late.

Dr. Iverson lived on an old quiet street, very different from Main Street, which was all I'd ever seen of Halstead. It was a big white house with old oak trees in front and a big yard. His office was part of the house, with a separate entrance.

There was a nurse sitting at a desk right near the door—she was probably the one I had talked to on the phone. I told her my name and she checked the appointment book. She didn't say anything about my being late. There were two women ahead of me in the waiting room anyway.

I took a seat on a sofa and started looking at a magazine, trying not to get nervous. I went over in my mind what I'd say to the doctor, then I tried to read and not think about it. I didn't know if he was young or old or what his attitude was going to be.

A woman came out of the doctor's office—she looked about twenty-five. She left with the older woman who was sitting across from me—I think it was her mother. The nurse took the other woman into the doctor's office, and about twenty minutes later she said the doctor could see me.

I followed her down the hall. She showed me a bathroom and told me to undress and put on a hospital gown. There was a stack of them folded on a shelf. After I had gotten into one I looked at my watch. It was almost quarter to five. I had told Mother I was going to the library after school but I didn't want to get home too late. The nurse took me into the examination room and weighed me. Then Dr. Iverson came in. He looked like he was in his sixties. The nurse stayed while he did the examination. It wasn't too bad, but I felt embarrassed. I was glad when it was over.

Dr. Iverson left the room and I got dressed again. Then the nurse took me to his office, which was down the hall. She left me there and closed the door behind her.

Dr. Iverson was sitting at his desk reading some papers. He smiled when I came in and asked me to sit down and right away he said, "Well, everything seems to be all right."

I sat down by his desk. I knew he was waiting for me to say something—he didn't know why I made the appointment. I told him I was afraid I might have V.D.

He asked, "Have you had contact with someone you know is infected?"

"I don't know."

"Have you had symptoms that have worried you?"

"No. But I knew it might—I thought I should see a doctor."

"Well, Miss Lenhart, on the basis of the examination I can tell you there aren't any signs of infection. But if your exposure was very recent that wouldn't be conclusive."

"It was five days ago."

"Then we'll have to do a blood test later. It's too early to diagnose now."

I started looking past his shoulder out the window at the trees outside. There were French doors with little windowpanes behind him. I was wishing I was outside too.

"I'm also worried about being pregnant."

"When did your last period start?"

I told him—all the stuff I figured out last night. He explained about the cycle and the days conception takes place, which I knew. He said he didn't think I could have gotten pregnant five days ago and I was probably worrying for nothing. He asked if I took the pill. I told him I didn't.

"I wondered if there was a shot you could give me."

"What kind of shot?"

"The morning-after shot?"

He smiled like he was a little amused. "Now how do you know about that?"

I didn't understand why he smiled at what I said. Maybe he thought I was too young to know anything about it.

"I heard about it somewhere. Or read about it."

"I don't think you ought to worry about that. I don't think you're pregnant—if you have the days of the month straight."

"I do."

I would have liked to get the shot anyway, if there was such a thing, but I couldn't think straight and when he didn't want to do it I didn't ask why. I just let it go.

It wasn't as bad talking to him as I had thought it

might be. He didn't say anything about my age or about my not being married. I had thought of buying a ring somewhere and pretending I was, but I didn't do it—I would have felt too strange. He didn't ask about my parents either, even though he must have figured I was coming without their knowing.

I asked him when I should get the blood test. He said I should wait six weeks, then call for an appointment. He didn't say anything about a pregnancy test. I figured I'd know in a few days if I was definitely okay and I wouldn't have to do anything about it. I guess he was thinking the same thing.

He didn't ask me any more questions. I could tell he thought everything was settled. I got up and went to the door. I was about to leave without telling him, but then I thought I should. It was the only chance I had to talk to someone who would understand about it and it seemed stupid to go to a doctor and then be too embarrassed to tell him what happened. Also I thought it might make a difference in what he did. If he thought I was going with someone I might get married to it would be a different story—he might think it wouldn't be such a tragedy if I was pregnant. He gave me a funny look since I just stood there by the door and didn't go out.

I said, "There's something I didn't tell you, Dr. Iverson."

"Yes?"

"I haven't told my parents or anyone. I was—the only reason I had to come here—I was attacked. It was the only time I could have ever gotten pregnant—it was the only time."

He looked down at his desk as if he didn't want to embarrass me by looking straight at me. I went back to the chair but I didn't sit down.

He asked, "What do you mean by attacked?"

"I was forced."

I was beginning to feel a little funny, sweaty. Talking about it made me think about it and remember things all over again.

"You weren't hurt?"

"He would have hurt me. He said he would. He had a knife. But I gave in, so. . . ."

I could tell his mood changed when I told him. He was as calm as ever but he seemed angry underneath. I thought he might have a daughter, or granddaughter, and was thinking about that.

"Where did this happen?"

"In a car. It was on a street with a lot of warehouses. There was no one to help me—it was deserted."

"What was you doing in a place like that?"

"He drove there. I was in the car with him."

"Now wait a minute. You say you drove somewhere with your boy friend—"

"Not my boy friend. I didn't know him. He said he was from out of state—"

"He forced you into his car at knife point, and drove—"

"No. I got into the car. He was acting all right at first—I couldn't tell. He was going to give me a lift home. But then he drove to this place—he pretended to get lost so I didn't know till it was too late—and there was no one around—he must have planned that—then he threatened me. I could tell there was something wrong with him. I was scared, the way he was talking and the way he looked at me. And when I saw the knife, then—"

"But you didn't go to the police?"

He looked puzzled, as if the story didn't make any sense to him.

"No."

"Why?"

"Well, I didn't want my parents to know."

That was all I could think of to say. He didn't say anything right away. I was afraid he was going to tell me I had to report it to the police.

Then he said, "You're very upset, Jenny."

"Yeah, I guess.... And right after—I didn't know what to do. I was just glad I got away. I didn't want to think about it. I tried to wash it away—get clean. Get it out of my mind."

Dr. Iverson didn't say anything. The office seemed so quiet. I looked around the room—there were books all along the walls. I thought he must be thinking about what to do. I thought maybe there were special pregnancy tests that could give very early when it was an emergency. He still didn't say anything.

"I've also been worried about—I've been feeling crazy. I thought you could tell me—if it's normal, I mean."

"What do you mean by feeling crazy?"

"I don't mean crazy—I've just been feeling bad, upset. I just sat around the house for three days doing nothing—afraid of everything. I couldn't talk to my parents, I didn't want to go to school or see anybody. I watched television all day and stared at things—I've gone back to school but I'm jittery all the time. I feel dirty—like I don't belong—like if everyone knew. . . ."

He was filling a pipe and trying to light it all the time I was talking. He seemed to be listening and waiting for me to finish but I didn't have anything else to say, so we both just sat there.

Finally he said, "You've been very worried."

"Yes."

"And feeling very guilty about this too, I think."

"I guess so. I don't think my parents would understand.

31

He turned in his swivel chair so he could look out the French doors. He puffed on his pipe. Then he starting talking—only he wasn't really talking to me, it was a lecture. All the time he was looking at the trees outside.

"You know, at your age it's common for girls to go through a period of confusion about sex. Nothing abnormal about it, even with the more open attitudes we have nowadays. You probably can't imagine the changes there've been since I was your age. In general, boys' drives are very strong in their late teens. That's why it's unfair for girls to act provocatively or to mislead." He stopped talking and started doing something with his pipe, tapping it. "Even today with the pill, girls never completely forget about the risk of pregnancy. Girls have very strong emotional involvements in their sexual relationships. It's not at all unusual for a girl to be ... pressured a bit. And perhaps to regret it later, bitterly, and to feel very guilty about it. To feel that she was taken advantage of. I don't mean to apologize at all for the young man in this situation. It's very unfortunate ... the girl is left with all the problems, as you know. But ... I feel I should point out to you, there's a great difference between a seduction and a criminal attack."

"I know the difference."

My voice came out very weak. What he said didn't have anything to do with what I had told him, but he was acting like it did.

"You see, Jenny, there's no evidence at all that you've been hurt."

"Yes—but that's only because I gave in. I *could* have been. I could have been killed."

He looked at his pipe. He seemed to be talking to it, not me.

"I assume you don't intend to report this incident to the police. Since you've waited so long."

"I don't know."

"I take it you didn't tell my nurse what your problem was when you called for an appointment. She said nothing about this to me."

I told him I didn't say anything over the phone. He looked at his watch—he said there was another patient waiting to see him. He asked me to go back to the waiting room and he'd get back to me.

I went back and sat on the sofa where I'd been before. There was a woman with a little boy in the room now. They were sitting across the room from me. The little boy came over and gave me a magazine. I said thank you—my voice sounded shaky. I felt embarrassed. I didn't know what the doctor was going to do. The buzzer on the nurse's desk rang and she went back into the office. I sat there waiting. It was already five-thirty and I didn't know when I was going to get home. I started thinking about the money—how I had to remember to tell the nurse that I was going to pay in cash and I could bring it Monday.

In a few minutes the nurse came back. She asked me to come over to her desk. She smiled at me in a businesslike way, but while she talked to me she looked down at the papers on her desk. She kept her voice low.

"Dr. Iverson has asked me to advise you that your examination reveals no evidence of injury. He can't be available for any kind of legal proceedings on the basis of the consultation. If you feel you need further care or tests in the future he suggests you consult your family physician. There'll be no need to contact him further."

She was acting like I didn't belong there—that I

had had a lot of nerve to come and see the doctor. I was so surprised by what she said I just stood there.

She said, "He won't bill you."

She didn't look at me. She kept her head down—staring at the blotter on her desk, as if she was embarrassed.

I felt stupid—I could feel my face getting hot.

I said, "Am I supposed to just leave?"

She didn't answer. I got my coat and went out. I was glad to get into the cold air—my face felt so hot. I was standing on the sidewalk when I heard the door open behind me, and the woman who had been in the waiting room came out, the one with the little boy. She came up to me and asked, "What happened?" She had a very concerned look on her face—she was young, but she was looking at me like a mother, as if I was a kid.

I said nothing happened. I just wanted to get away. I couldn't look at her or talk to anyone. I started walking down the street, heading back to Main Street.

I tried to get calmed down on the bus. I knew I was going to be late for dinner—I was supposed to be home at six. I didn't want to be upset or act funny when I came into the house. I tried to push everything about Iverson out of my head—kept thinking I'd never have to see him again, or his nurse, so it didn't matter. There was a boy about eighteen sitting across the aisle from me—I think he used to go to the high school. I began to get the feeling he was staring at me. Maybe I looked upset. I changed my seat and sat behind the driver till we got to Central.

I was a half-hour late, but it worked out fine. Dad was in the kitchen making a salad. He had gotten home late too and Mother had decided to take a bath and relax before dinner. Dad was in a good mood and started asking me about school. He thought I had stayed late at the library—he said I shouldn't work too hard trying to catch up or I'd get sick again. He asked me what I was studying. I said English—just to say something.

"What are you reading now?"

"*Hamlet.*"

"I saw a performance of that in Central Park with your mother. About ten years ago. Do you like it?"

I said I did. I don't know why I said *Hamlet*—I couldn't think of what I was really doing in school—it was the first thing that flew into my mind. I had never read it—we were supposed to later in the year. It was very strange, Dad washing things in the sink and asking me questions about *Hamlet*—he seemed to remember it pretty well. I thought of something to say and he didn't notice anything wrong. I felt crazy talking to him about it.

Mother came downstairs with her hair up, wearing slacks and a sweater with a design, almost like a ski sweater. She said there had been a lot of kids in for measles shots and it had been a hard day, but she was in a good mood—she started laughing about a kid who bit Dr. Grinnell. They had wine with dinner—one of Dad's clients had given him a bottle. I asked for some. It helped, made me more relaxed while they were talking about Rob. He's definitely coming home next weekend. Then they decided to go to the movies. They asked if I wanted to come—I could tell Mom had decided to forget about our argument.

35

I said no, I was going to study and go to bed early. Before they left she gave me a kiss on the cheek and said not to work too hard. She said she had seen a skirt at Silbey's and she was going to get it for me Saturday if I liked it. She was in a good mood, very happy for some reason—she seemed so young in that sweater. She was wearing beautiful perfume.

I was glad when they left. I had been expecting trouble all the way home from Iverson's and instead everything was fine and they didn't notice anything funny about me, but I felt crazy talking to them.

After they left I took a bath and lay down on my bed. I didn't know what to do. I thought about calling Clara and telling her everything that happened and asking her for advice. Iverson hadn't told me anything about what I should do if I was pregnant—all he did was tell me to wait. And if I was, I wasn't supposed to go back to him. After going through all that I was no better off—it was as if I hadn't gone to a doctor at all. It drove me crazy to think of him—all the time acting so calm while I "confessed," smoking his pipe, and his nurse, acting so cool and above it all in her white uniform, treating me like dirt. And I stood there and did nothing, like a jerk. I would have liked to go back and tell them both what I thought of them. I imagined going back and slapping the nurse, then going into Iverson's office and getting him too, sending that stupid pipe of his flying across the room. But all the time I was thinking about it I just lay on the bed doing nothing, breathing hard, almost crying, remembering different things about the whole stupid afternoon. I was tired, but not sleepy—I knew I couldn't get to sleep. I played some music, but it didn't calm me down—it made me more jittery. I went downstairs and turned on the tube. There was wine left on the table. I had a glass—felt better. Didn't want to finish the bottle in case they might notice so I got some gin and mixed it with orange juice. It really helped calm me down. About ten-thirty the phone rang. It was Johnny Fenton. I was scared for a minute before I realized it was him. He invited me to the basketball game in Waymouth, but I said I couldn't because I had been out sick and my parents said I had to stay home over the weekend. I was happy he called, kind of surprised too. I asked him to Clara's party next Friday. He said I sounded different—guess it was the gin. I said I was just sleepy. I hung up and watched the tube for about an hour, the end of a movie, then went up to sleep. Didn't hear them come in.

I woke up early. The radiator in my room was rattling—it got very cold again during the night. Except for that the house was quiet. Dad works Saturdays, but he doesn't have to get to the office till ten. I put on my bathrobe and sat by the window. No one was up yet. Everything was still. No cars on the street. I was trying to think what I should do. I thought about Clara, Miss Elias at school, even thought about calling Rob.

After a while the Rosser kids came out to play—the early birds of the neighborhood. They had on snowsuits, one red, one blue. Mrs. Rosser brought their tricycles out of the garage—she was still in her bathrobe. She must have been cold—I could see her breath in the air. The kids rode down to the end of the block and back, then they dumped the tricycles on the sidewalk and started running around their front yard. I could hear Karen yelling something—some kind of nursery song. I started thinking about Rita Stahley and how we used to be such good friends before she "went berserk" as my father would say.

I decided to go see her, but I waited till ten to call. Rita slept late Saturdays, at least she used to, and I wanted to be sure she was up. But even at ten her mother answered and had to get her out of bed. It was a while before Rita came to the phone—she sounded surprised to hear from me. I said I needed help with my History. I wanted to have an excuse in case I changed my mind when I saw her. She said to come over.

It felt strange walking over there. I used to go by the houses on Fairway Street practically every day going to Rita's house, but I hadn't been out her way for a long time. We were very good friend till about ninth grade, then we started not getting along. She lost interest in a lot of the things we used to talk about—she started acting much older, and she would make sarcastic remarks about things I said when I didn't expect it. It was as if she turned into a different person, very tough and sarcastic. Before that she had been just the opposite, shy and sensitive. She felt out of it in school and didn't fit in too well. She really used to suffer. I could tell, but something must have snapped. Now nothing bothered her anymore.

She had run away from home quite a few times, with her parents reporting it and the cops looking for her and everything. The first time she was out of school six weeks—she had gone to visit her brother who was in college in Maryland. He had sent her back but she took the long way home. She returned to school for a couple of weeks, then she ran away to her great grandmother's house in Ohio. Her great grandmother called her parents and this time they went out to get her. She didn't know they were coming. The last time she really ran away—not to a relative's house. She was in about fifteen states and ended up in Georgia where the cops picked her up and sent her home. Now she had to see a psychiatric social worker every week—she had had a hearing and that's what the judge ordered. It was in family court, not a regular trial.

Rita wasn't a sympathetic person, not like Clara. She was always calling people "morons" and sometimes she was snotty to me too, but I could tell she didn't mean it because I was always friendly to her during "the bad times" when she was sensitive and didn't have many friends and she remembered it. She knew a lot for her age—that was one reason I thought of her—and I knew she wouldn't be shocked like someone like Clara would be. Also I knew I could trust her not to tell anyone—for one thing she wasn't that friendly with anyone at school. She always held herself apart. In the lunchroom it looked like she was serving a jail sentence and didn't want to mix with the inmates. Not that I didn't trust Clara, but she had a lot of friends besides me.

Rita was in the kitchen having breakfast, and she wanted to stay there and eat. Her parents were somewhere around the house so I couldn't talk—I just had to listen to her. She was talking about college. She said she was dying to get away—away from "the local morons" as she put it. She was applying to Harvard, Yale, everywhere. She said she'd gotten terrific grades since junior year but she was afraid her record before that was going to do her in. She wanted to be a biologist. All of this was new to me. I didn't know if she was exaggerating about her marks or about her college prospects. Once she had told me her parents weren't going to send her to college because they couldn't afford it—they had spent all their savings on her brother. Now she was talking about the most expensive schools in a very casual way while she ate.

Finally I said I had something to ask her and I didn't want anyone to overhear. We went up to her room. I told her the whole story, what happened with the guy and then all about Iverson yesterday. I was hoping she'd know a doctor I could go to.

She acted just the way I knew she would. Nothing surprised her. She listened to it all without saying anything. Then she said, "Why did you get into a car with a creep like that?"

"He didn't look like a creep. He looked like anybody else."

She didn't say anything—I don't know what she thought.

I told her I didn't want to go to another doctor, but I thought I'd better.

She said, "You're not kidding. You might have V.D."

"I know."

"Well, all you need for that is a shot of penicillin. Are you late?"

"No."

"Did you have it already?"

"No. Next week."

She said, "I'd be more worried about that than V.D."

"Do you know if there's a shot I could get? If I was pregnant?"

"I don't know. Didn't you ask the doctor?"

I *had* asked Iverson about a morning-after shot, but he had acted like it was a figment of my imagination.

"Look, do you know a doctor who might be able to help me?"

"I know a doctor. I had to go to one after my last trip. My parents were afraid I picked up something."

She didn't talk much about what happened on her "trips," and never said anything about sex. I knew a lot could have happened, but I didn't know.

"*Did* you pick up anything?"

"Nope."

"Was the doctor okay?"

"I don't know. I didn't like him."

"Did he give you a hard time?"

"No, but he acted like he was doing me a big favor, then he sent my parents a bill for fifty bucks."

"For one visit?"

"Yeah. I didn't get a shot, Jenny. I don't know anything about that. It might be the same as an abortion and some doctors wouldn't do it."

"Well, what if a kid ten years old got raped. They'd have to give her something, wouldn't they?"

She just shrugged. "I don't know. You're probably supposed to get it right away."

"Yeah, but I didn't."

Rita didn't say anything. I felt a little annoyed, but naturally I couldn't express it. Then she said, "This doctor's expensive. I don't know what he charges now. Do you have any money?"

"What I made this summer."

"Can you get it?"

"Sure, if I have to."

She said, "You know what I'd do if I were you?"

"What?"

"Go to a clinic and get the V.D. tests. They'll be free that way and maybe you could get a pregnancy test too—or a shot—if you told them what happened."

She had a pamphlet with a list of clinics. She looked all over her room for it and finally found it. She said she got it from a girl who had been at a runaway shelter in the East Village in New York and got it there. The clinics were all in New York City, none out where we were. She also got me the name and phone number of the doctor she had seen—his name was Seymour. He lived in Armingdale.

❀ ❀ ❀

I was only at Rita's an hour—it seemed like longer. I didn't feel good when I left, but I didn't want to go home. I went to the library and sat around in the reading room for a while. I was still thinking about how Rita had acted—I didn't know whether it was normal, or good, or what. I could hardly believe I had told her. I didn't know if her advice made any sense—whether someone else would have told me something completely different. A lot of people thought Rita was wigged out and the last person to ask for advice. I would have liked to talk to someone with their feet on the ground, someone "normal," like Clara or Miss Elias, see what they would say. But in another way I didn't think someone like that would understand—it didn't seem like the kind of thing that would happen to them. It seemed like something that would only happen to someone who was different, an "outsider," the way I felt in school the other day. I guess that's why I thought Rita would understand.

There was a pay phone in the front hall of the library. I was going to call Dr. Seymour and try to get an appointment. I knew I should, and I was thinking I wouldn't have to tell him the whole story and go through that again, but I dreaded the idea of another doctor. I waited around trying to decide, then I left without calling him.

❋ ❋ ❋

When I got home Aunt Helen and Laura were in the living room with Mother. They were the last people I expected to see. They said we were all supposed to go shopping at Five Oaks. I didn't remember anything about it. Mother said she told me last night. They'd been waiting an hour. Mother didn't know where I was—I had left for Rita's without telling her. I said I had been at the library. Laura was looking at me cross-eyed, probably still mad about last Sunday when I didn't go over there. I said I couldn't go shopping, I had too much homework and I was getting over the flu. Mother started kidding me. I said I wasn't going. She said, "Oh, come on," and she grabbed my arm like she was going to drag me with her. All of a sudden I got mad. It was as if I freaked out. I pulled my arm back and shoved her away. I don't know how I could have done it. She almost fell I did it so hard. She looked surprised, very embarrassed in front of them. I ran upstairs. I was almost crying.

She came after me up to my room. I couldn't tell how mad she was—she looked bewildered. She said she wanted to know the meaning of it—I told her to leave me alone. She said I should apologize to Aunt Helen and Laura—I said I wouldn't. Then I called her some names she never heard before. Her mouth fell open—she stood staring at me like she had turned into a statue. All of a sudden I was scared. I wasn't before. I didn't know why I did such a terrible thing. I don't know what they heard downstairs. The door was open and I wasn't keeping my voice down. Thank God Dad wasn't home. Mother looked at me like she'd

43

never seen me before, then she went out. I would have locked the door if I had a key.

I don't know if she's going to tell Dad. Maybe she won't. I don't know what he'd do—maybe kill me.

Mom came up later and said she and Dad were going to the Andersons, and there was something in the refrigerator if I wanted to heat it up for dinner. She said she wasn't going to tell him. She said I had humiliated her in front of Helen and Laura and she didn't know what to do about it or what to tell them. She said she didn't know what she'd done to deserve that, she had never said anything like what I had said to anyone, and she would have died before she spoke that way to Grandma, no matter how mad she was. I didn't say anything—I didn't know what to say. I could hardly look at her. She said it was up to me to apologize and explain. She waited, but I didn't say anything. Then she left. I heard Dad come in later. I almost died when I heard him coming up the stairs. But he went straight to their room and then a little later I heard him go downstairs again, then they went out.

❀ ❀ ❀

I woke up early again, it was still pretty dark out. I couldn't get back to sleep. I started looking around the room, staring at the rug by my bed as if I'd never seen it before. I kept staring at the design as if I wanted to memorize it—curving vines, flowers, leaves, green and different colors. At first everything looked gray, then when it got lighter the colors came out. I would have liked to sink into it and not have to do anything but hide there until everything was better, but there I was stuck in my own world and my body. I felt terrible—hopeless. I looked outside the front window. The Rosser kids' tricycles were dumped on the sidewalk, on their sides. I kept staring at them, I don't know how long.

Maybe I was wrong about Iverson. He's a doctor, he's had a lot of experience with people and he must know a lot about sex being a gynecologist. He's not a quack or anything—he has a nice office, a good practice, all those books. Maybe the reason he kicked me out was he figured I didn't have to let it happen, and the nurse thought the same thing when he told her. I didn't have to take the ride. It's true—Clara wouldn't have. Rita was surprised when I told her. Iverson probably thought I was asking for it and then trying to get him all involved. I could have gotten away, or at least tried harder. I didn't put up much of a struggle, I didn't even get hurt, like Iverson said, except for the bruise on my leg.

Mother and Daddy must have warned me a million times not to take rides. When I started walking to school by myself without Rob they were always saying it. They made me very afraid of kidnappers; I would never have gotten into a car. When I hitched a ride to the shore once with Rita and Daddy found out he was furious. Mother was mad, but I thought he was going to hit me. He kept after me—I promised him I'd never do it again. Robby, too—he said it was okay for boys, but not safe for girls. Everybody warned me about it. Even *him*—when he parked the car by that building he said he knew why I took the ride—he said I shouldn't act so innocent. Maybe it looked that way and anyone would think so, then when I tried to back out of it he got out of control and that's why he acted like that—because I was leading him on. He didn't seem crazy before, just a kid who could have been in high school—nothing like a criminal.

I don't have amnesia about it, but some of it's fuzzy in my mind. He said he was from around here, he said he was going to college in Morrisville, then he said he was from out of state, but he knew all the teachers. I'm positive about that, I remember it—he was talking about Corry; he didn't like him. It's true I'm not innocent. I was interested in him, a little attracted to him to be truthful—I was thinking of asking him to Clara's party. If we had gone out maybe we would have started making out, so in a way he was right—I wasn't that innocent. I was warned not to take rides. He only had a pocketknife, like a lot of people might carry on them, he didn't even open it. He put it on the dashboard—why would he do that if he was going to use it? I could have grabbed it. He was just trying to scare me. Why was I such a coward? I'd give anything if I had another chance, I'd do everything so different. I could have acted like I knew what I was doing, like Clara would have done, told him to go to hell, or just gotten out of the car and run away. I could have screamed, but I didn't. I just gave up, like a kid going off to get a spanking, thinking there was no use. And crying, begging—wish I hadn't—wish I hadn't given him the satisfaction. No wonder he laughed at me, called me those names. I don't know why I did it. If someone asked me I couldn't explain why I acted the way I did.

❀ ❀ ❀

I saw Mother. Went down late for breakfast and she came into the kitchen for something. I stayed in my room most of the day, but I had dinner with them. I didn't help her cook but I did the dishes after. She acted like everything was normal, but I can tell she's still mad. I don't think she told Dad anything.

❀ ❀ ❀

I apologized to Mother tonight. I heard her go up to her room. Dad was downstairs watching television. I told her I was sorry and I didn't mean anything I said. I said I'd never do it again. I said I loved her and I knew all the things she did for me, that I didn't want to give her any trouble and I'd never do anything to embarrass her again. She said it was all right, but we didn't really make up. She didn't want to hug me or anything. She's still mad, cold. The atmosphere is terrible.

❀ ❀ ❀

School was okay. At least I went. Felt lousy and looked lousy. I had that "outsider" feeling again—like I was looking at everything through a pane of glass, not really in it.

47

I made a mistake in chemistry—Corry let me do my make-up work in his second period lab since I had a study. I broke a test tube I was washing in the sink and Corry thought it had acid in it, which it didn't—he started yelling at me in front of everyone. They were all doing another experiment. I didn't answer him back, then he started making jokes at my expense—he said it was dangerous in there, it would be hard to get fire insurance with girls like me in the lab, etc. I just ignored him while he kept talking—my face was probably red as a beet. After class he stopped me at the door, said, "Hey, what's the matter? You know I've got to keep people on their toes in here." I guess he had expected me to laugh. I told him I'd been sick and I was having trouble catching up. I was upset—I didn't like him suddenly bringing attention to me and everyone staring at me.

I started to feel weird in History, that "outsider" feeling again. I was thinking about sex—not sex really, but some things I did when I was little, playing "doctor" with a couple of kids down the street. Mother found me and got very upset. I was so ashamed, felt like a rotten freak next to her, didn't know if they'd let me into kindergarten. I felt crazy thinking about that while the history class was going on. I was afraid Miller was going to call on me. She didn't. I thought I felt cramps, but nothing happened.

I went over to Grandma's after school. I got the idea all of a sudden—didn't want to go home. She was glad to see me, started hugging me, then right away started yelling at me for not coming over more. She's wearing all black again—like she used to in Sicily. I told her she should wear something with a little color—she has beautiful dresses. She looked at me like what did I know—didn't bother to answer me.

She was cooking as usual. I sat in the kitchen and she gave me some anisette cookies. I felt jumpy at first but then it went away. We talked a little in Italian. She talked about Laura. I told her about Robby coming home (she knew). She asked about Rita—still thought she was a shy little kid. Her house was so peaceful, it seemed like a different world. I felt funny, as if she thought she knew me but she really didn't, but then it seemed like nothing much had changed. I started thinking about the old days when I went to the house on Carmel Street every day after school and she took care of me when Mom started working. It was from when I was seven till junior high so Grandma and I were close then. Once in a while Rita came too. Mother said I should encourage Grandma to speak English, but it didn't work out. After Grandpa died (he wasn't Italian) she lost all her wish to be modern and American and she went back to the way her mother was—started speaking Italian, staying in the house doing a lot of cooking all the time, wearing black clothes. She became old fashioned all of a sudden. Mom thought I could help snap her out of it, but I couldn't. She stuck to her old (new) ways and I had to adjust to her instead of vice versa. She wanted to speak Italian and sometimes she forgot I didn't know it. I picked up a lot—that's why it came easy to me in school and Miss Farrand thought I was a genius. She didn't know I was part Italian at first since I don't have an Italian name, and she didn't know how I picked it up so fast. It is a beautiful language, very full, with a smooth rhythm, very clear, and the spelling is exactly the same as the pronunciation. Compared to it English is full of "shadows"—letters in the words for nothing (as in "ghost" or "window"). Before school I just thought of it as Grandma's personal language. I was almost surprised to hear other people talking it and to see books written in it.

Grandma was making eggplant. When she finished she sat down at the table with me and started crocheting—she's making a sweater for the family's baby upstairs. I asked her to show me and she taught me to chain and single crochet. She gave me some red yarn and let me practice while we talked. She did hers so quickly—the sweater really grew while we were talking.

When I left she kissed me and called me her little angel like she used to. She put her hands on my head, like giving me a blessing. That's how she meant it and that's how I took it.

❀ ❀ ❀

I got home too late to call the doctor—I didn't even think of it until I was home. Daddy was working late. Mother ate watching television and I ate out in the kitchen—guess she wanted to avoid me and vice versa. I didn't want to see her. When I'm "good" everything's fine, but when I do something wrong she hates me, doesn't act like a mother at all.

It's nerve-wracking waiting for my period. Checked the calendar again to make sure I got it right. I think Grandma would love me no matter what I did, but there are some things she could never understand— wouldn't even believe.

❋ ❋ ❋

School was okay. Rita came by in the morning to walk me over. Mother came up and told me she was there. I could tell she was surprised. It was only about eight and I wasn't ready but I finished getting dressed fast. When I came down the stairs I heard them in the kitchen. Mother asked how school was and Rita was saying, "It's boring, I'm not learning anything, and I don't like the people." It made me nervous to think of them together—I never knew what Rita was going to say.

On the way to school Rita asked me what I'd done, if I'd call the doctor or what. I told her I hadn't had a chance to do anything yet. She was more considerate than I expected—she didn't say I was crazy or anything. I told her I was a day late. She said sometimes she was a week late and once she skipped a month. She also said that nerves can make you irregular, which I'd heard. I knew a day late isn't anything—it's just that I'm usually on time.

I saw Clara lunch period. She was talking about the party Friday. She wants me to come early and help her. I told her I had asked John Fenton. She wanted to know if she should ask Rita. I didn't know what to say—Rita was always cutting her up behind her back to me, but maybe she just envied Clara and would love to go. Nobody asked her to things anymore. I said it was up to her, but she shouldn't expect Rita to bring anyone. Don't know what she's going to do.

❀ ❀ ❀

I want to make a shawl for Grandma for Christmas. I'd like to make it red—which would look beautiful with her hair—but I know she'd never wear it so I'll get blue, a nice shade, not too bright, so she'll really wear it.

After school I walked over to Lamston's to buy the yarn and crochet directions. When I was in the store something happened—nothing important, but I got scared for a minute. A guy was standing at one of the counters with his back to me and I thought it was him. He had exactly the same kind of shirt on. I froze for a minute, and was about to go out of the store the back way so he wouldn't see me. Then he turned and I saw it wasn't him, didn't even look like him. I don't know why I thought it was. The shirt I guess.

Going home I passed a kid in a skeleton outfit on Grove Street. I didn't even get it—then I saw another one in a fireman outfit and I suddenly realized it was Hallowe'en. That's how out of it I was.

Mother was acting the same at dinner, not talking to me. Daddy did most of the talking—about a client he drove around all day. He thought he wasn't really in the market for a house, just looking, but he wasn't sure so he couldn't say anything. The man gave him a hard time too. There was nothing Dad hated worse than someone wasting his time, but he could never be sure if they were or not. Mother finally said something aimed at me—she said she'd never seen anyone change as much as Rita had, in looks and manners. She said, "She used to be such a lovely girl." Kids were ringing the doorbell all through dinner, trick or treating, and I was only too glad to leave the table and get the door. Mother had bought candy and nuts and stuff. There were ghosts, skeletons, witches—I knew who they all were. The Rosser kids came by with Mrs. Rosser. Joey was a cowboy and I don't know what Karen was supposed to be—some kind of clown I guess. Mrs. Rosser asked me to babysit next week and the kids both got mad—as if I didn't know who they were.

I tried to study up in my room—started the lab report for Corry, but got bogged down and couldn't concentrate so I didn't finish it. I began to wonder if anyone was having a party. No one asked me and I didn't hear anyone talking about one. I played some music and started the shawl. It was hard to figure out the directions from the book—they must have been written for mathematicians. I finally figured out the first part and started the bottom—it's about an inch wide already. Doing it gave me something to concentrate on, kept me from worrying so much. Took a hot bath before I went to bed. Mom and Dad stayed up late—I could hear the television downstairs.

❀ ❀ ❀

I woke up in the middle of the night in a sweat—I had a nightmare about "Baron Samedi." I was in bed (in the dream) and I heard the floorboards creaking outside the door. I went to check and there he was in the doorway, grinning at me. He was just like I remembered from Rob's crazy stories—seven feet tall, wearing a shiny black satin suit and a black top hat, and yellow gloves, yellow shoes, and carrying a yellow cane. He pulled out a calling card, talking in a lilting calypso voice—"Hello, little garbage, I am Doctor Death and I see you are alone tonight"—smiling all the time. I almost had a heart attack when I saw his face.

The last time I had a dream about him I was about eight. Robby told me all those stories. I don't know how he heard them—I never heard anyone else talk about "the Baron." He was supposed to be a voodoo man in Haiti but Rob said he could go anywhere at night. He told me some frightening stories about different things he did, trying to scare me. I had some terrible nightmares and Dad made him stop.

It must have been Hallowe'en that made me have that dream. It scared the hell out of me until I woke up and realized where I was. I thought of waking up Mother and asking her to sit and talk to me awhile but then I remembered I couldn't.

❋ ❋ ❋

School wasn't too good. Had an English test I didn't study for—I'd forgotten all about it. Also I had to tell Corry I didn't have the lab report—he made some remark.

Before History Eddie Farrell came over and told me Barini said I could work next summer if I told him now. I didn't know what he was talking about for a second, then I remembered telling him I wanted my job back for the summer and he had said he'd ask for me. Then he said, "I see you've got a new boy friend." I didn't know what to say—I wasn't sure what he meant. Then he said I was a fast worker, getting a ride home like that. He had seen me leave Lenny's with him. It was the first time I had thought about it—that Eddie was working that night and could have seen us. I tried not to show anything, made a joke about being a fast worker.

❊ ❊ ❊

I woke up during the night again. It was about one o'clock. Right away I started thinking about my period. I hadn't thought about it much all day but all of a sudden I felt panicked about it. I started thinking about how I hadn't called another doctor, I'd just let more time go by, trying to ignore the whole thing. I turned on the light and looked at the calendar again and went over all the dates. It made me feel better, like nothing could really be wrong. I tried to go back to sleep but I couldn't. I suddenly felt like I had to throw out the clothes I was wearing when it happened—get them out of the house. They were all clean, not torn or anything, but I didn't want to wear them again or have them around. I decided to get rid of my sneakers, too—everything but my jacket. I went downstairs to the kitchen and found a bag and put everything in it. The next day was garbage collection day and the cans were out by the curb. Even though it was late I went outside and put the bag in one of them, under some stuff.

I walked back to the house just in time. Dad's car came into the driveway. He had been out playing cards and he had had a few drinks—I could tell because he was driving very slowly and carefully. Naturally he was surprised to see me out in the front yard in my bathrobe—it was two o'clock. I said some papers had gotten out of the garbage cans and were blowing around the yard and I saw them from my room and came down to get them. He believed it. I could tell he had won by the way he was acting. I asked him how much and he said about fifty. As soon as he got into the kitchen he went for the refrigerator. He made a sandwich and offered to make me one too. I said fine—I didn't want to go up to my room again and he was in a good mood. He started telling me about the game—all the cards he was holding, how much was in the pot, what all the players did—all the details, even though I didn't know how to play poker. Then he took out his wallet and put his money on the table, and started counting it as if he didn't know how much it was—he was right the first time, almost fifty. He gave me ten and said I could get anything I wanted. I knew he was in a good mood but I didn't expect that. He finished his sandwich and got a glass of milk. He wanted to stay in the kitchen and sober up a little before he went up in case Mother was still awake.

It was strange seeing him like that—he was usually so businesslike. In one way I felt like laughing, but in another I hated it. It didn't seem like him. When I was little I really got upset one New Year's Eve when he got looped—I thought he wasn't really my father. I liked him to act like his usual self. I asked him some questions about poker but he kept assuming I knew how to play. He didn't answer anything, just kept telling me about the great way he played. My Uncle Ralph was there (Mother's cousin) and he lost. Dad seemed delighted about it. He was acting incredibly childish. I asked him if he wanted me to make him some coffee before I went up but he said, "I don't need any coffee." Then he started laughing. He didn't say anything about me being up so late on a school night.

※ ※ ※

I finally got up my nerve—not to call the dreaded Dr. Seymour, but to go to the clinic. In the back of my mind I was thinking I'd go Saturday, but I woke up early—I didn't feel sleepy even though I went to bed so late, and I had the idea in my head that I couldn't put it off anymore, I had to do something right away. I had the list of New York clinics Rita gave me. I'd been to Radio City and the museum and places like that but I really didn't know my way around. Luckily one of the clinics was on 27th Street, and I thought I could find it without much trouble since I'd been to the Empire State Building on 34th Street.

I felt scared, but not as much as I'd been about calling Seymour. I got dressed, then I went downstairs and had breakfast as if I was going to school. Mother was in the kitchen; Daddy was still sleeping. I waited around to see if Rita was going to come by again—she didn't. I left the house at eight-thirty, then I walked over to Fairway so I could get the Bayville bus. I'd gone that way with Clara a couple of times so I wasn't worried. It was a funny feeling on the bus, knowing school was about to start and I was going the other way. I was thinking about what I'd say if anyone asked me why I wasn't in school. I got off at the stop past Bayville and got the train. The round-trip ticket was almost four dollars.

The train got into Grand Central Station about ten-thirty. There was a lot of stalled traffic on 42nd Street, and people were rushing around. I walked a couple of blocks, then I decided to take a cab. I had the rest of the money Dad gave me so I figured I'd have enough for anything that came up. It was too long to walk and I didn't want to lose my nerve along the way. I gave the driver the address—303 Ninth Avenue. He didn't say anything, just put the meter on and started driving.

There was a lot of traffic for a few blocks but then it thinned out. In about ten minutes he let me off at the corner of Ninth Avenue and 27th Street. I didn't know which building the clinic was in but I wasn't going to ask him. I just stood there on the sidewalk until he drove away.

It was a quiet part of town for New York, at least compared to Grand Central Station. There was an old church on the corner, and then next to that some modern buildings with terraces. It looked like a housing project. The top of the Empire State Building peeked out from behind one of the rooftops. The building next to the church had an even number, so I crossed the avenue. The buildings on the other side weren't as modern, except for a school. The one on the corner looked like a factory or jail. I was hoping it wasn't the clinic. It wasn't. I had trouble finding 303—in some ways I didn't want to find it. I went past the school and two other buildings and finally came to 303. It was an old brick building with a yard and trees in front, set back from Ninth Avenue where the traffic was whizzing by. I walked into the driveway. There weren't any people in front but the lights were on so I knew it was open. There was a statue of a man holding a bayonet outside the entrance. It was a World War I memorial.

I hadn't been worrying too much on the train or even in the cab, but when I got right up to the building and read "Department of Health" I felt like forgetting it. It looked cold and very institutional and I thought it would probably be a thousand times worse than Iverson's. At least he had a nice office. I didn't know what kind of people would be working there or what kind of questions they'd ask me. Then I thought about all the reasons I had to go and I got up my nerve and went in.

There were quite a few people inside. Some people were waiting in the lobby and there were others passing by going in and out of the different rooms. The first people I saw were men, but then I saw some women too, just as many.

No one paid any attention to me when I came in. There was an information booth in back—two women in nurses' uniforms were sitting there talking. There was a sign near them that said, "V.D. Clinic." The sign gave all the directions. There was a stack of plastic tickets with numbers, like bookmarks, on a table. I had to take one and go to the women's waiting room and wait for them to call my number. I took a ticket—I got the number 39—then I looked around and saw the entrance to the women's waiting room. It was off the lobby, right near the information booth. I went in and sat down on one of the chairs lined up against the wall. There were three women there, all of them older than me. Two of them looked about twenty-five. The other one was younger—she had on jeans and wore her hair long and straight; she looked like she was in college. She was reading a pamphlet. There was another one on the table, so I picked it up. It was all about V.D. It said the treatment was confidential and minors didn't need their parents' consent, and it gave some facts about V.D. It was printed in English and Spanish. I started reading the part about syphilis. It said it was a very dangerous disease which could cause blindness and death, but it could be cured if it was treated early enough. It said the first symptoms were sores, like cold sores. I didn't have anything like that, but then it said people didn't always notice them, especially women, and they could go away without treatment and you'd have syphilis without knowing it. I began to get a strange sick feeling, as if I couldn't believe I was really there reading about a disease like that which I might have. I had to stop reading. I looked around the waiting room. It wasn't like Iverson's—no carpets or easy chairs or pictures on the wall or anything. There was linoleum on the floor, plastic chairs like in a bus stop, and the walls were painted bright blue. They seemed too loud, as if they were yelling "V.D." at you. The people weren't that quiet either. Right outside the door I heard a man saying, "Well, I don't think you have anything, but you'd better come back next month." Naturally it wasn't a secret to anybody what it was all about, but I couldn't get used to it. All around the building you could hear numbers being called out.

The women ahead of me got their numbers called and in about fifteen minutes the nurse came in and called mine. I followed her out into the lobby. She went into another room toward the back, behind the information booth. She was in a hurry—didn't look back to see if I was following. She had on a blue uniform, something like a nurse's uniform, but maybe she wasn't a nurse.

She went into a room filled with people and desks—about eight desks jammed into a little room. There were people like her, in uniforms, behind the desks and others on the other side, men and women. I saw the college girl from the waiting room talking to someone.

The woman I was following went to a desk in the corner and told me to sit down. She took my "39" ticket and put it in a tray with some others, then she started looking at some papers and cards on her desk. It wasn't exactly a private office, but in a way it was because everyone was talking and no one was paying any attention to anyone else. I looked out the window—there were some kids passing by outside, probably from the school I saw on Ninth Avenue.

The nurse asked my name and address and started filling out a card. I gave her my right name, but I made up an address in the city. I didn't know if they'd take me if they knew I was from out of town, and also I didn't want them to have my address. It was supposed to be confidential, but what if they made a mistake. All I'd need would be for Dad to see a letter to me from a V.D. clinic.

"Phone number?"

I said, "I'd rather you didn't call me at home."

"You call here for the test results. We need it for the record."

I didn't know why they wanted it if they weren't going to call. I thought maybe if they found out you had V.D. and didn't come back, they'd try to find you. I made up a phone number—Murry Hill something. She just wrote it down.

"Married?"

"No."

"Date of birth?"

"February sixteenth, ninteen fifty-nine."

"You're sixteen?"

"Almost seventeen."

"Symptoms?"

"What?"

"Have you had any symptoms?"

"Oh. No."

She didn't say anything. I don't know what she was thinking. She got a card out of a drawer and wrote a code number on it and gave it to me. It had information about the clinic on it—the hours it was open, the phone number to call, and spaces for appointments.

"That's your permanent patient number. Don't lose the card. You give that number when you call for the test results."

She gave me a test tube with "39" marked on it.

"This is for your blood test."

She got up and I followed her back to the waiting room. She told me to wait until they called my number again. There were two women in the room, not the same ones as before. I didn't know if that was all the questions they were going to ask me. I waited—didn't read. After a while a man came in and called my number. He had on a white doctor's coat and he was carrying a clipboard. I went with him down a long hall past some offices. At the end there was a room where they did the blood tests. A nurse was sitting at a table there with a wire rack full of blood samples in test tubes. She took my card and the test tube and told me to roll up my sleeve. I did. I sat down on the chair by her table and she tied a rubber tube around my arm and told me to make a fist. I looked out the door down the hall.

She asked, "What's the matter?"

I told her I didn't like needles.

She said, "Not too many people do."

It didn't hurt that much—I didn't watch. After she got the sample she put the test tube in the rack with the others and took the rubber tube off my arm. She put a piece of cotton on the inside of my elbow where she'd given me the needle and told me to bend my arm. I did.

"Keep it bent."

"Okay."

"Don't forget your card."

It was just like an assembly line. The man with the clipboard came back and called a woman in a green uniform. He told me to go with her. She took me around the corner and down another hall to a dressing room. She said to get undressed from the waist down and she gave me something that was like a bath towel, but made of paper—she said to wrap it around me like a skirt and then go into the doctor's office. It was right across the hall from the dressing room. I was getting nervous but I did what she said and went into the office. She was there. She told me to sit on the examination table and wait for the doctor. She left and I sat there staring at the wall. There was a big chart of the female reproductive system across from me so I looked at that.

In a couple of minutes she came back with the doctor. I hadn't seen him before. He was about forty and he had some kind of accent. I can't remember what his name was, although he told me when he came in. He sat down at a desk against the wall and started looking at some cards. He must have had the card the nurse filled out when I first came in.

"You're Miss Lenhart?"

"Yes."

"You haven't been here before?"

"No."

"You have no symptoms?"

"No."

"No rash, no itching, no sores?"

"No."

"Have you had contact with someone you know is infected? Someone who is being treated here?"

"No. I don't know if the person is infected."

"But you want to have the tests because of possible exposure?"

"Yes."

"Are you allergic to any medication?"

"I don't think so."

"Have you had penicillin?"

"I don't know."

He wrote something down. I had the feeling that was all the questions he was going to ask me.

I said, "The only time I'm worried about was about ten days ago."

"You mean your only exposure was ten days ago?"

"Yes."

He wrote something down on the card.

"Do you know about the incubation period for syphilis?"

"No."

"It won't show up on a blood test this early. You'll have to come back. We can do the other tests now."

That was all the questions. They had the whole routine down to a science. He gave me an examination, just like at Iverson's, then I got dressed and went out to the waiting room again. He came out in a few minutes and sat down by me. He told me they had done a smear test for gonorrhea and it was negative. They were going to do another test for gonorrhea that took longer—I was supposed to call them in a week to get the results. He said they'd give me the results of the blood test for syphilis then too, but it would probably be negative and I should get another one in a few weeks. He asked me again if I understood about the incubation period for syphilis. I said I did. He told me not to lose my patient card because I had to give them the number when I called for the test results. He was acting very nice and I had the thought I should ask him about a pregnancy test or even ask him if I could talk to him privately somewhere and tell him the whole story, but I didn't have the nerve. I felt relieved the test was negative and I was dying to get outside. I felt like I'd been in there a year, but it was only a half-hour or so.

I started to walk back to Grand Central Station. It was only about 11:30 so I had plenty of time to get home. I didn't know how often the trains ran—didn't think to look at the schedule when I was in the station. I walked up to 34th Street and then east, past Madison Square Garden and Macy's and a lot of stores. It wasn't too cold, but it was windy and felt chilly—fall weather. I stopped in a coffee shop to warm up and get something to eat—I hadn't eaten much breakfast. I had the pamphlet from the clinic with me and I read it there—I was trying to remember the main things since I didn't want to bring it home with me. It said the same thing the doctor told me about syphilis, that it took time for it to show up in blood tests. I also read the part about gonorrhea. It said it could cause you to be sterile and sometimes women didn't have any symptoms so they didn't know they had it. It could be cured with penicillin. It described more about what each disease could do to a person if it wasn't caught early—I couldn't read too much of it. When I put the pamphlet away I saw an old man across the counter staring at me. I guess he saw what I was reading even though I was trying to hide it. I went out and started walking again. It was lunch hour—the streets were full of people.

❋ ❋ ❋

I wish I had walked the rest of the way, but New York made me nervous and I felt like I could get lost on those crowded streets even though I was close to the station and ought to know where I was. A cab stopped and let somebody out right near me, so I decided to get in and get back as fast as I could. I told the driver I wanted to go to Grand Central Station.

I got a talkative one. He told me all about the one-way streets and how he had to go down Fifth and circle around to get back uptown. He got me a little nervous because I didn't know what he was talking about or what he was doing as he turned into different side streets. He was young—he was wearing an army fatigue jacket and he had long hair. He said he wasn't from New York. He started talking about the lousy weather in New York, then he said the rest of the country had worse—he said he drove around the country once and ran into tornadoes in the midwest and a hurricane down in Florida, and once he was in California when they had an earth tremor. He said, "You can keep it."

I was getting nervous for some reason—I didn't know what street we were on. I grabbed the door handle—my hand was all sweaty. All the time he kept talking to me through this thick plastic partition. He asked me where I was from. I said Bayville. I began to feel like I was trapped in the cab. He asked me what I was doing in Manhattan. I told him to let me off.

He said, "I thought you were going to Grand Central."

I said it was okay and paid him and got out. I didn't care what he thought. I was shaking. It got me nervous being in the cab, him talking to me like that, maybe trying to start something, me not knowing where he was going. As soon as I was out on the sidewalk I felt okay and it seemed stupid.

I walked to the corner and found out where I was—39th Street and Lexington Avenue. He had been going the right way. I got to 42nd Street and Grand

Central all right. I only had to wait about ten minutes for a train. I threw away the pamphlet in a trashbin on the platform.

A strange thing happened on the train. It was rattling along, everybody reading their newspapers, and I had nothing to read so I started looking up at the ads along the top of the car. One of them said, "To Report a Rape." It gave a phone number and said, "A policewoman will help you." I stared at it, then I looked away at all the other ads—for bourbon, Household Finance, Speedwriting, a lot of other things. It all seemed unreal—my head was spinning. I looked at the sign again and tried to memorize the number, then I had the feeling I'd forget it before I got home so I wrote it down.

Dad wasn't home. He'd left a note saying he had to drive out past Amityville and show that house he was trying to unload. He said not to wait dinner for him. I was glad I didn't have to see him and make up something about how school was if he asked. I went upstairs and took a bath and put on slacks and an old shirt. There were a lot of things in my mind but mostly I was relieved—at least I had gotten up the nerve to go to the clinic. I wanted to tell Rita but I didn't want to call her. She said her mother listened to her phone calls on the extension—I didn't know if it was true or if Rita was exaggerating, but I decided I'd better go over. I was about to leave when the phone rang. It was Mother. She wanted me to come over to Dr. Grinnell's and bring her an umbrella. It was starting to rain and she couldn't get a ride home. I said I would.

When I got to the office Mother was helping a kid on with his boots and telling him some kind of story. He was laughing. It was strange seeing her at work—so efficient on the phone and talking to Grinnell about somebody's symptoms. She seemed to like the kids—it was nothing like the way we got along. Grinnell said I'd really grown up the last year. He hadn't seen me since the summer before junior year.

We walked home along Rosemont Avenue. It wasn't raining hard, but it was windy and once the umbrella went inside out. I told her about Dad's note. She said Rob had called her at work—he was bringing a girl friend with him for the weekend and it looked like I was going to be sharing my room with her. She was excited about seeing Rob. She said Grandma was happy I had been to see her and she was glad too. I mentioned the shawl I was making for Grandma; Mom seemed surprised—guess she thought I was too selfish to go to the trouble.

When we got home Mom made some tea—said it would take the chill out of our bones. I sat in the kitchen with her. She said she wanted to talk about Saturday. She asked if I'd been seeing much of Rita lately. I said a little. She said Rita had changed and she hoped I wouldn't spend too much time with her—she knew Rita hated her parents (and would tell anyone about it), that she'd run away from home again and again, and that she had a generally negative attitude about everything. She said she didn't think Carol Stahley (Rita's mother) was so bad and she felt sorry for her having a daughter like Rita. She said in her opinion Rita was a curse to her parents no matter what they had done. I said didn't she ever wonder what made her that way—maybe Mrs. Stahley wasn't as nice as she seemed and she made Rita act that way. She said, "Who could make anyone act like that?" Even though it was a slight argument and she kept on about Rita (she called her hair a rats' nest) I could tell she wasn't mad at me anymore.

She said she was glad Dad wasn't going to be home for dinner because she didn't feel like cooking. She had a frozen pizza in the refrigerator and she put it in the oven for us. She showed me some chairs she got at an auction last week—they were down in the cellar. Four dining room chairs—old and beat up, the varnish all chipped, but she said they were good wood. She was going to refinish them and make needlepoint covers for the seats. She said Rob would be starting a house of his own someday and she wanted something nice to give him. I said I'd help her with the chairs. She refinished a lot of old furniture—got things cheap and made them really beautiful. I never thought the things would turn out, but she was right, they always did. I used to help her with the sanding and waxing. I knew she brought it up because she wanted us to do something together, like we used to.

We started sandpapering one of the chairs and she brought down the pizza. She sat in the old sofa with the springs sticking out of it. We were getting along better than in a long time but it was strange because of the whole day and her not knowing where I'd been. She started talking very seriously. She said what had happened had made her do a lot of thinking. She said she knew we weren't as close as we used to be, I had been growing away from her the last couple of years and she didn't know why or what to do about it. She brought up what I said one time when we had a fight—that she loved Robby more than me. She said it wasn't true, but she felt she understood him better. She said after he was born she always wanted a daughter, and when she got one she expected me to take after her, the way she took after Grandma (until Grandma changed). She said at first I did, but then I changed when I got older and she didn't understand it. She said Rob was more like her than I was. I knew what she was talking about, but I didn't know what to say. She said she wanted me to tell her when there was something on my mind. I just said I was sorry about the fight on Saturday, I didn't mean it, and it would never happen again.

She said she still wanted to take me to get that skirt she saw in the store since I didn't have enough things for school. She said she saw Laura's closet when she was over there last week and she had about twice as many things as me and at least she could afford to get me the skirt. I told her I didn't want to be in a clothes race with Laura, didn't want to compete with her or be like her. Even though Laura was supposed to be so wonderful she was selfish and no one ever mentioned she nearly flunked math every year because she could hardly add—it had been that way since third grade with her. And she never went to see Grandma unless she felt like eating. I once saw her eat three plates of ravioli over there in about ten minutes. Mother groaned and said, "Oh, no, let's not start on Laura again," but she was laughing.

Very tired—guess it's catching up with me, not sleeping. Don't know if I did the right thing—at least the test was negative. I wish I'd talked to the doctor, told him the truth, asked him what I should do if I was pregnant. I couldn't bring it up. I think he would have helped me more than Iverson, but maybe not. Maybe he would have said it wasn't his job.

I've been thinking about Mother, what she said about us not being close, me not taking after her. It's true, but I can't say it to her. I never wanted to be like her—I never hated her like Rita hates her mother, but I always wished she was different—stronger. Sometimes I didn't respect her. She lets Dad win every argument—he always has the last word. She started working because they were worried about money. Dad hadn't sold a house or gotten any commissions for three months. They were arguing a lot about money—he kept saying she should economize more. What was she supposed to do, steal groceries from the supermarket? Mother hadn't had a job since she got married and she was afraid to look. Then she got the receptionist job in Grinnell's office. I remember the morning she started work, she was so nervous she was shaking. I felt sorry for her but it scared me to see her like that. I hated her for being weak. I felt rotten for feeling that way because she was only doing it to help the family and how could I look down on her.

Four days late. Everything will be better once I get my period—everything will be normal again. Sometimes I think I have cramps, then it goes away and I think it was just my imagination. I wonder if Daddy sold the house. I have to call the clinic next week and find out the other test result, ask them when I should go back. Use the code number on the card. Rita said I should have asked him for a pregnancy test, told him what happened. Maybe so—it's easy to say when it's not you. Walking over to Rita's, the skeleton glowing in the dark in the Crowley's garbage can —I didn't know what it was at first. I wonder why they threw it out, some kid would have wanted it next year. I couldn't have gotten pregnant. It's probably nerves. I should have asked the doctor at the clinic about the morning-after shot—I'm sure I heard about it somewhere. Haven't talked to Robby for a long time. Wonder why he's bringing home a girl. Maybe I did the dates wrong on the calendar—maybe I was a week off and I'm not even late—worrying for nothing. I have to write an excuse for school, sign Mother's name. I really love her—I feel so bad when she hates me—so lonely. I must have been crazy to say those things to her—filthy. I was so mad I could have killed her, everybody. I get so angry. Thank God she didn't tell Dad. I wonder why they have that phone number to report a rape. Who would call it? I wonder what that cab driver thought—I was so scared all of a sudden—thank God I don't have anything. Even if I do they can cure it. Syphilis could make you go blind. That man in the coffee shop saw what I was reading. They can give you penicillin. Sometimes I'm afraid I have it and they won't be able to cure it—stupid. I'm afraid I'll never be the same again. I'm not a bitch, none of the names he called me, not garbage. . . . It was my fault in a way, but not like Iverson said.

I went to school Friday and Clara's party that night. She wanted me to help so I went over early. It was nice to see the Andersons again—Mrs. Anderson said she'd missed me. She had baked bread for the party, for sandwiches—the kitchen smelled fantastic. I didn't realize how long it was since I'd been over there.

The party was okay, but not everybody came.

Clara's parents were strict and there was never any smoking or drinking at her house so some kids only went there as a last resort. Probably there was another party somewhere and some of them went to that. I couldn't tell if it bothered Clara. Rita was there, with a boy named Sam. I was surprised Clara asked her and even more surprised that she came. She sat in the corner talking to Sam most of the time. Don't know how she met him. He looked about seventeen or eighteen. He seemed very different from her—not sarcastic, very serious.

Johnny came late—he had to wait to get his father's car. I sat next to him in English junior year but I had never seen him outside of school before. We talked a lot—it was that kind of party. He wanted to go over to Ron Kasabach's house after for beer, but I told him I couldn't because I had to get home to see my brother when he came in. I'd never been over to Ron Kasabach's house and I didn't know who went to his parties. John was nice—I always thought he was—but I had that "outsider" feeling talking to him, thinking how he didn't know any of the things on my mind. He asked me if I wanted to do something next weekend so I guess he had a good time.

I was feeling a little out of it, but not having a bad time, then about ten-thirty Sonia Cris came with Judy Young and a guy I didn't know, her brother Bob Cris, and Eddie Farrell. I didn't know who Sonia was with—I didn't know she knew Eddie. They had been at another party. Sonia was acting pretty snotty, not just coming so late, but looking around like it was a dull party. She told Clara she was starving—almost as if to say straight out that she only came for the food.

Eddie came over while I was talking to John—he said I'd better see Barini soon if I wanted the job because it was going to be hard to find jobs for the summer. Then he said, "I didn't expect to see you here with Fenton. What happened to that other guy?" He was only kidding around, but I felt funny and I was afraid it was going to show. I was afraid he was going to say something else, call me a fast worker like he did in school, or a pick-up—something someone would ask questions about and then he'd tell the whole story. I don't know what I said—I acted like it wasn't that important. I was nervous with Sonia around too—if she heard something she'd try to make something out of it. As soon as I got a chance I went up to Clara's room—I didn't feel good and I didn't want to bump into Eddie again, or Sonia. I was thinking Eddie might know a lot of things—if the guy had been in Lenny's before, or if he'd been back, or if anyone there knew him. But there was no way I could ask him without making him think about it more and I was hoping he'd forget it.

John drove me and Rita and Sam home—he let me off first since I had to be home early, but when I got in Dad told me Rob wasn't going to get in till Saturday. I was still glad to be home early—I wouldn't have had a good time with all the things I was thinking about.

❀ ❀ ❀

Strange day, so much new. Rob and Barbara got in after lunch. He said they'd been driving seven hours—they left Ohio at six-thirty in the morning. We spent all day talking—the whole family—and we had a great dinner. Barbara's sleeping in my room tonight. I gave her my bed and I have the cot.

74

I didn't like her at first. She seemed snobbish, but then I realized she was just nervous about meeting Mother and Dad. She's quite pretty, almost as tall as Rob. She's a psychology major. She has a sister my age, also in her last year of high school. Robby has grown a beard. It makes him look completely different. I don't like it but I didn't say anything. He didn't say anything about it either. He acts like he's always had it. He's going to spend Thanksgiving with Barbara's family in Denver—that'll be the first time without him. It sounds quite serious between them.

Barbara and I talked a little before we went to sleep. I would rather have been by myself, but there was nothing I could do. She offered to take the cot, but I didn't switch. She said she was glad to meet me at long last because Rob often spoke about me. I wonder what he said. She doesn't wear make-up— none—she just brushed her hair and washed her face and she was ready for bed. I was surprised she just wore plain blue pajamas—don't know what I expected. I wonder what her and Rob's usual sleeping arrangements are. Maybe they would have gladly gotten rid of me. I wonder where they spent Friday night—kind of funny their sudden change of plans. Nobody asked about it.

She talked a lot about Rob. It sounds to me like she completely idealizes him. Naturally I didn't say anything to add a sour note.

After we stopped talking I didn't fall asleep right away. I didn't know if she was awake or asleep. I thought of asking her what I should do if my period didn't come. She was a college girl so she'd probably know more than I did. Also, since she was a psychology major, she might know about the "outsider" feeling and that fit of rage I had against Mother.

75

❀ ❀ ❀

I woke up early. I had cramps and I thought my period had finally started, but it hadn't. I felt so let down. I had really thought that was it. Barbara was still asleep in my bed. All I could think about was my period. I should have seen another doctor right after Iverson. I kept putting off calling the one Rita told me about, Dr. Seymour, and now more than a week had gone by. I was six days late and I was never late. I began to feel panicked, then I pushed it away. It happened like that a few times—I suddenly got scared, then I got control of myself and didn't think about it.

❀ ❀ ❀

Robby and I went for a drive—he was supposed to teach me to drive this year. We drove down to the school field but I didn't feel like having a driving lesson. We just parked by the baseball field and talked. I told him I liked Barbara. He said he was serious about her—I knew it. They had gone to see Grandma in the morning, also over to Uncle Jerry and Aunt Helen's house so Barbara could meet them and Laura.

He said Grandma told them Jimmy Calissi is going to become a priest. I was surprised—I didn't think Jimmy was that religious. He always lived next door to Grandma so I saw him a lot when I stayed with her, and he was a friend of Rob's. Jimmy was the kind of kid everyone liked, but I never thought he was that serious. I asked Rob if he believed in God.

He said, "Why do you ask that?"

I said, "I wanted to know what you think."

He said, "It depends on how you define God."

I said, "Do you think there's a plan in the world for each person? Do you think things happen for a reason, or is everything by chance?"

He wouldn't answer. I asked him, "Do you think terrible things happen to people for no reason, or is it a punishment for something?"

He said, "What do you mean?"

"Just what I said."

"But why are you asking?"

I asked him if he thought there was such a thing as sin.

"What do you mean by sin?"

"Do you think if someone does something wrong they have to suffer for it forever? And it can't ever be forgiven?"

He said he didn't understand why I was asking so many strange questions when there weren't any easy answers to them.

There was a question I would have wanted to ask

77

Rob, but I couldn't. He wouldn't have answered and he would have wondered why I asked. I wanted to know if boys could get so desperate for sex that they would force someone, even against the person's will. I couldn't imagine having the feeling that strongly. I didn't ask him any more questions. He didn't take me seriously, so there was no point to it.

We drove back for dinner. Dad talked about the real estate business, and Rob and Barbara talked about school. They had met in a European history class. Barbara and her whole family like to ski—they're close to the mountains in Colorado. I listened to everybody talk and didn't say much. They left soon after dinner, started the long drive back to school. Had my room to myself again. Tried to study for the chemistry test, but couldn't concentrate.

❀ ❀ ❀

Had a lousy day in school even for Monday. Forgot my gymsuit and had to tell Miss Elias. She said I'd already missed two classes and three meant a C if not a failure, which depended on some skills tests she was giving next week. She was really acting snotty—very stern, like a prison matron. I wasn't in the mood to just take it and quietly say, "Yes, Miss Elias" like she expected.

I said, "I doubt if colleges care that much about marks in gym."

She said, "Oh, yeah? Why don't you try failing it and see?" Miss Tough.

I have to make up the class after school Thursday.

Also I got a 65 on my history test—I'll be lucky if I get a B- now. All day long I was thinking about the weekend and Rob, and feeling bad. He really hurt my feelings the way he was talking to me—trying to act like he was so much older than me, not just four years. I noticed it happening ever since he went to college. He seemed to think he was a father figure to me and I was just a kid. He couldn't talk to me except to ask me questions about why I said something, as if I was crazy. His beard seemed to make it even worse. He acted older and very calm, almost like a religious leader. He seemed to think that, being the younger sister, I had always been guided and protected by him, and he had always helped me with my problems. But when I was younger one of my worst problems was him. He would often tease me and push me around. If it hadn't been for my parents he probably would have maimed me or driven me crazy. Now he had completely forgotten about that. I wished he would have told me what he thought instead of always asking me why I asked.

At lunch Sara Shomer asked me if it was true I was going with a boy in college who picked me up in Lenny's. I don't know how she heard about it. It must have been Eddie. He made that crack at the party so maybe he was mentioning it all over. I told her I did meet a guy from college, but we weren't going out anymore. Then after eighth period Clara came over to my locker and asked about it too. She had heard it from Sonia, who was telling somebody else in the lockerroom before phys ed. It was the kind of thing no one would have said anything about if some other girl had done it, but the joke was supposed to be that I was shy and now I was supposed to be a pick-up. I told Clara it happened the night she was supposed to meet me at Lenny's—it was so damn cold I took a ride home from a boy who went to Morrisville College, but we never went out after that. I tried to make it sound a little like it was her fault for not showing up in case she felt like acting disapproving. She didn't say anything but I think she was a little surprised—I don't know what she thought. Maybe she didn't think it was such a big deal.

I wanted to go to Eddie and ask him not to spread the story around anymore, but I couldn't. I had to act like it didn't bother me. I hoped it would die down. All I needed was for it to become a standing joke, like when Arnie Cooke fell down the stairs and everybody started calling him "Slide." They still do. No one knows it, but it wouldn't be exactly funny to me to be called a pick-up. I guess Eddie only meant to tease me, or maybe rock the boat for me with John—Pretty rotten—but I don't think he meant to make me miserable. I always thought he was a nice kid. Maybe it'll die down if I act like it doesn't bother me.

I walked Rita home after school. I told her I had taken hot baths and everything and I was still waiting for my period. She said I should have asked for a pregnancy test while I was at the clinic. She was surprised I hadn't called Dr. Seymour yet—she asked me what I was waiting for. I said I was going to call him. Then she said I was probably worrying for nothing. She was often a week late and once she had skipped a month and it didn't mean anything. She met that guy she had brought to the party in the library of all places, a few days before. He's from New Jersey and had to start school at Bayville High his senior year so he doesn't have many friends. Like her—that's what she said. She didn't exactly calm me down but she was the only person I could talk to.

When I got home I tried to do my English, but I couldn't concentrate so I turned on the tube. Mother came home and found me staring at an old B movie. She asked if Dad had been home or called. He hadn't. She said she didn't know where he was, but he probably had to work late so why didn't we go and get the skirt and get something to eat at Five Oaks. We drove out there and got it. It's beautiful—blue—the nicest I have, and as she said I can use it for college. We went to a new place by the five and ten and got soup and sandwiches. We talked about the weekend. She likes Barbara but she said she's sorry she lives so far away. She seemed a little sad, probably thinking about Rob, or maybe just tired. She asked me about Clara's party since we didn't get a chance to talk all weekend. I said it was okay. She talked about Clara—she likes her more than any of my friends. She asked about school and I said everything was okay. Even though I couldn't tell her anything, I still felt glad I was with her.

Dad still wasn't home when we got back. I took a long hot bath and then studied my English, but I didn't get much done. When the letters on the page started to look like little bugs I figured it was time to give up. I got into bed and then I heard Dad come in and they had an argument. He was mad she didn't make dinner and she said she didn't know where he was or if he was eating out or what. He had been back to the house while we were out. I heard him yelling—he said he wasn't going to eat another frozen tv dinner again. I hated to hear him yell at her—made

81

me feel panicky with all the other stuff on my mind. I don't know what she said. It went on a while, but then it died down.

I felt on Mother's side. I couldn't get to sleep. I started thinking about her and remembering times in the past when we were close, and times when I was sick and she took care of me, the kind look on her face even when she was tired. She took care of me when I had pneumonia and then she got sick and there was no one to take care of her. Grandma wouldn't leave her house and Dad had to work. Mother was always in bed asleep when I got home. I went into her room and watched her sleeping. Sometimes I brought a sandwich in there and ate watching her. Sometimes I was afraid she wasn't going to get well. I didn't know what I would do without her. She looked so weak. Her face was the most beautiful thing in the world to me. Now I felt so lonely being cut off from her. I started thinking it was my fault for not trusting her. She was a good mother and she'd try to understand, but I was afraid to give her a chance. I was seven days late. I knew I should have called Rita's doctor, but I couldn't do it. I had started to call him, but I felt paralyzed—I couldn't do it.

I was lying in bed with the lights out, but I couldn't fall asleep or stop worrying. I didn't know what to do, I was so confused. I started crying. I didn't know it was so loud. Mother heard me, she must have been passing by the door. She came into my room and asked me what was wrong.

She sounded so understanding, but I couldn't tell her. She sat on the bed and put her arms around me and tried to smooth down my messy hair. She asked me what was wrong. I kept crying, holding on to her, but I couldn't tell her. I said I was worried about school. When I calmed down I said I wasn't doing too well and she shouldn't expect much my next report card. I said the pressures were terrible senior year with all the competition to get into colleges. It was all true in a way since I *was* screwing up in school and I might as well get them ready for my report card. She said I shouldn't worry that much about marks, all she and Dad wanted was for me to do my best. I could tell she didn't understand why I would get so upset about it since I never had before.

She brought me a glass of milk and said she'd sit by me till I fell asleep. She put a towel over the lampshade and sat by the bed and worked on her needlepoint in the dim light. She has so much patience, it gave me a very peaceful feeling. She didn't say anything about the fight with Dad, she just talked in a quiet voice about this and that. She said she had done needlepoint and embroidery since she was a kid. She got in the habit when she listened to radio shows and soap operas on the radio—"The Shadow," "The Lone Ranger," "Our Gal Sunday." In one way her life was like mine, in another so different. With television I never thought of embroidering or anything. I just stared at the screen like a little zombie. Wonder why Grandma never taught her to crochet.

I could see her embroidering and her face in the dim light. She looked tired but she kept talking—think she was trying to comfort me. I told her I was sorry we didn't get along better. Ever since I was about twelve we couldn't agree on anything and it got worse every year. She said she didn't always get along perfectly with Grandma. One reason she didn't like to cook was that Grandma made such a big thing of it and used to boss her around in the kitchen. I was getting sleepy. I told her I appreciated her getting the skirt for me. She said I shouldn't worry and to go to sleep. I felt peaceful with her there and I did go to sleep—don't remember her leaving the room.

❀ ❀ ❀

School was all right. Not really, but I tried not to let it get to me. I didn't feel like seeing anybody, skipped lunch and went to the 103 study hall and just sat there. I couldn't concentrate in any of my classes, but I didn't get called on. Even Corry left me alone. I was so glad when the bell rang. After homeroom I left 303 like a shot and went to my locker and left before anybody got there. I didn't feel like standing around like a jerk while everybody was talking and kidding around—I felt so out of it.

Dinner was all right. They must have made up from last night. Nobody seemed mad at anybody. They talked about Rob and Barbara. Mom was nice to me, didn't say anything about last night. I guess she thinks I'm upset about school, like I told her.

I had to babysit at the Rosser's and I was almost going to call Mrs. Rosser and say I couldn't make it. Then I thought I might as well go. That was where it started. I couldn't believe it. I was putting Joey to bed and then I got a feeling, but I was afraid it was my imagination. Then I went to the bathroom and checked and it was true. After a week. I was incredibly relieved, almost couldn't believe it—almost thought I was imagining it. It still hasn't hit me completely. Now I won't have to see a doctor. I can forget about calling Dr. Seymour, and worrying about how to get there, and how to pay for it, and how to cut school, and how he might act, and what he might say—the whole thing. I still have to go back to the clinic, but I'm not afraid of that.

I wish I could talk to someone besides Rita. I feel so lucky. This whole thing has been like a nightmare—you don't even realize how bad it is till you wake up.

❁ ❁ ❁

Had a really happy day in school.

I told Rita after school. I didn't make too much of it with her—I never know how she's going to act. She just said, "Oh, hey—" like, "What do you know?" as if it wasn't that important.

I'm going to try to get back on the right track now—be better to Mother, try to fix things up at school, everything. Maybe this will make me a more understanding person and I won't ever look down on people in trouble.

I knew I was worried, but I didn't realize how big a strain it was on me, and it went on a long time. I can feel the difference now that it's gone.

Everything is okay now physically—soon I'll be back to normal mentally, too. It'll be as if it never happened.

I feel great!

❁ ❁ ❁

Today Rita was sitting alone in the cafeteria reading and wearing sunglasses. It looked so funny, as if she was traveling incognito and she thought no one would recognize her. I almost bust a gut laughing.

Clara said she'd been wearing them for weeks. It shows what a fog I've been in. Clara must think I'm crazy—in a good mood for a change. I was thinking about when I went over to Rita's house and told her the trouble I was in—she was wearing those sunglasses. I was so out of it with worry I didn't even think it was strange to tell her the whole story with those dark blank eyes staring at me.

Clara and I went over and sat at Rita's table. There were plenty of seats. We talked about the party. Rita said she's going out again with that boy—Sam. I wonder if she really met him at the library. John came over and asked me if I wanted a ride home after school—he had the car. I told him I had to make up a gym class for Elias. He sat with us and we talked until the bell rang. Rita was reading *The Theory of the Leisure Class*. She said it should be *Our Town*. She told us about an experience she had in Arkansas. My first thought as she started talking was: Is this all a lie? She said she got a job washing dishes in a diner because she was hungry and didn't have any money. This was in a place called Two Forks or something like that. She met a lot of people there, including the sheriff. He came in for coffee every morning and he spotted her as a runaway right away. He knew she wasn't from Arkansas with her accent, and he knew she wasn't eighteen as she had said. He tried to get her to call her parents but she kept sticking to the story that she was from Texas and eighteen. Finally he said she'd have to leave town or go to the local church and think about what she was doing. She told him she didn't have any clothes for church, but the owner of the diner wanted to keep her there and his wife lent her some clothes. Rita went to the Methodist church in that outfit, but after the second

Sunday she took off after the service and got on a Greyhound bus. She said she didn't want to stay in that town with everyone taking such an interest in her. (Funny.) I didn't know she ever got as far as Arkansas, but it was close to Missouri where her grandparents lived—it was probably that trip. I wasn't sure she was telling the truth, but she whipped out a snapshot they had taken of her outside of church. There she was in a flowery hat and some clothes that didn't fit her too well and the same sunglasses she was wearing now. When I saw the picture, especially the sunglasses, I started cracking up all over again. The whole table was roaring. I mentioned that I was thinking about giving a party around Christmas—a lot of kids I know are starting to get along and it would be great if everyone got to know each other better before graduation because then everyone breaks up.

John walked me to history. He was acting nice—I told him all my worries about school, with Corry and so forth. He doesn't like Corry either. Sonia saw us going into history and naturally she couldn't let it pass. She said, "Oh, how'd you pick him up?"

I said, "The same way you act like an idiot—it just comes natural."

She was surprised I answered her back since I was cowering from her at the party, but she tried to act like it didn't bother her. She said, "I know it comes natural to you. Where else do you go besides Lenny's?"

I said, "Why? Are you looking for some other places to try?"

She just walked away—she couldn't think of anything to say. I was glad I told her off but it made me nervous. I thought the "pick-up" joke was dying down, but she had to bring it up again. I was still glad I put her down instead of laughing nervously as if I didn't know what she meant.

I finally did that second lab report for Corry in study hall, then after school I made up the gym class for Miss Elias. She didn't have any remarks to make, so I guess she was satisfied with my gymsuit and sparkling sneakers. After that I went home, got dinner ready so Mom wouldn't have to worry about it.

Before bed I started reading the book for my book report in history—on Harriet Tubman. I'm going to try to get an A and make up for that test I failed. It looks interesting so maybe I can get inspired and do it.

Got inspired to write a poem:

Maybe we won't have to hear about Robby's
    great brain
At dinner which gives me such a pain.
Because I am just as smart as that great genius
    of a nineteen-year-old brother
And I'm going to prove it to my father and
    mother.

And also Grandma! And all the relatives! And Barbara too! And last of all the towering genius Robert himself!

Right after school by my locker a couple of guys made remarks about "pick-up." Why do they think it's so funny? George Rill said it like it was so clever. I didn't hear everything he said, just as well. If only he knew how unfunny it is to me to hear it for the tenth time. I tried to look bored so he'd cut it out. I thought I heard Bob Cris's voice, didn't want to look over. I felt rotten—mad—but I couldn't do anything. It bothers me, but not like before.

It was a good day except for that. Had a long talk with Rita lunchtime—she said some strange things, really surprised me. We might double Saturday night. Talked to Clara and John too. Sometimes that "outsider" feeling goes away—feel so happy then. I feel peaceful and sort of hopeful, as if things are going to get better.

❦ ❦ ❦

I went to Lenny's. I did it just so I'd know it didn't bother me. I also wanted to ask Eddie to stop spreading that dumb story around—I was hoping I could think of how to say it without sounding too concerned about it. He wasn't there. Dorothy was working and we talked awhile. She said her husband was laid off and she's working fulltime now and he's taking care of their little boy. She said Eddie wasn't coming in.

Barini was in his office, and I went back and told him I wanted the summer job. He said he'd hold it open for me if I'd promise to show up as soon as school closed and not disappear to Europe for the summer. He said he'd be turning down a lot of kids for me. (As if it was a job in the Library of Congress.) I told him not to worry.

I didn't want to hang around so I left right away—had a funny feeling passing by the cars in the parking lot, seeing the neon sign and the highway where the traffic was rushing by as always.

I got home and I was going to get started working on my damn history, but Mom called me from work. Aunt Helen and Laura were sick with the flu and I had to go get groceries for them and go over and help. They were in bed, Uncle Jerry had to work and couldn't get home till late. Mom said there was money in her dresser drawer and I should use that. I went to the A & P near their house and got some things I thought they could use, including grapefruit, orange juice and soup, which we always had when we were sick in our house. I almost broke my back carrying it—forgot how heavy all those canned things were.

When I got to their house I rang the doorbell and had a long wait until Laura finally came to the door. She was in some grubby pajamas and looked terrible, but she was glad to see me—she looked surprised too. She said Aunt Helen was sleeping. The doctor had been there and he said they both had bad cases of flu and they'd just have to rest and wait for it to take its course. Laura said she felt incredibly weak—when she heard the doorbell she thought she was going to have to crawl to the door. I went up to see Aunt Helen and tell her I was there coming to the rescue, but she was sleeping so I just let her be. I told Laura to go back to bed and I'd make them something to eat and bring it up.

I went to the kitchen and found some trays and all the other stuff I needed. Made the same thing for each one—a glass of orange juice, a whole grapefruit which I peeled completely, every section, some onion

90

soup, a Spanish omelet with five eggs which I split between them, and some tea.

I woke up Aunt Helen and told her she had to eat. She was happy to see me. She had expected Mom to come after work. She said not to come too close or I'd catch it and be flat on my back for a week. I said I was going to eat a grapefruit and take some vitamin C to ward it off. She said she didn't know if it worked.

Laura was in bed staring at the ceiling in her dark gloomy room when I got to her. The illness really subdued her. She had the radio by her bed but she said she got tired of listening to it. When she tried to read she got a headache. I put the tray by her bed and sat with her while she ate. She described all her symptoms and asked me if it was what I had when I was out of school. I said more or less. I wish. She was worried about her mother. She was very close to Aunt Helen.

With Laura so weak and helpless I could see the human side of her much better. When she was well and parading around with all the new arrivals to her closet all I could see was red. She said, "Thanks for coming over and taking care of Ma, Jenny," then she started crying. She said she was afraid her mother was going to die. I don't know why, since it was only flu. Maybe it reminded her of the time Helen was in the hospital for the operation and everyone thought it was serious. I reminded her what the doctor said and also that she had the same virus and she knew she was okay except for that. They had exactly the same symptoms. She seemed relieved, as if she hadn't thought of it before.

I told her I had to go, but I'd bring them more stuff if they needed it the next day. I brought the trays down and cleaned up. My aunt had eaten most of what I made for her and she had fallen asleep again. I didn't wake her up to say goodbye.

❀ ❀ ❀

I was working on my Italian composition after dinner when I got the idea of calling Rob. I suddenly felt like I had to talk to him. A boy answered the phone in his dormitory and said he'd get him. Rob was in his room studying (he said) so he came on right away. At first he thought it must be an emergency for me to be calling him long distance so I had to calm him down and tell him everyone was fine and the house hadn't burned down. I said I just had to call and tell him I liked Barbara and I was very happy for them. I said I was in a fog all weekend because of some things in school and I didn't get a chance to tell him how I felt. He was surprised to hear from me, but I think he was glad I called. I told him I was going to miss him Thanksgiving, the whole family would. I told him some of the things I was thinking about our talk in the car. I said he had to realize I was getting older too, not just him. He didn't become nineteen and all the time I stayed five. I told him it drove me crazy when he would never answer my questions, as if I was too young or stupid to discuss anything with him. I said if he didn't know the answer to something, or didn't want to tell me, he should just say so instead of asking me so calmly why I was asking. He said he wouldn't do it anymore. He said he didn't realize he did it and he didn't know it bothered me. Since I was on the subject I was going to remind him about the "Baron Samedi" nightmares he gave me when I was small and about the time he shut me in the closet "for fun" when I was in kindergarten—to give him something to think about, so he would realize he wasn't so mature and perfect compared to me—but I didn't want to keep criticizing him. I said I had to hang up since it was long distance. He said, "Is that really all you called for?" I said it was. I told him I really loved him and I said give Barbara a big kiss for me if he could remember to do it. He laughed and said he would. I said "Good night, mio fratello bono e caro." He said Barbara liked me!

Something bad on the ten o'clock news. Wish I hadn't seen it.

Stopped in to see Laura and Aunt Helen again after school. Went to the library on the way and got a book for Laura, *Great Expectations*. Didn't have to get groceries because Uncle Jerry drove to Bohacks last night and got everything.

They looked much better. Aunt Helen said she was going to make dinner. I didn't stay too long, just gave Laura the book and sat with her awhile. I told her I had talked to Robby, and we talked about him and Barbara. She said she thought Barbara was okay, but not the kind of girl she expected Robby to get serious about. I asked her what kind she expected. She said she couldn't explain it. I told her I might have a party after Thanksgiving. She seemed surprised—probably didn't expect me to invite her since she was a year younger, not to mention the other reasons.

She said she was afraid she was going to fail algebra and asked me if I would help her with it if she came over after school. She said she'd only stay a half hour and really pay attention. It was amazingly humble for Laura. I said it would be okay with me.

I thought of asking her what she heard me say to Mom, if anything, that time we were all supposed to go shopping together and I blew up, but I decided not to. She had never said anything about it and neither had Aunt Helen. Maybe they didn't hear anything, or if they did they had decided it was better to forget it.

Walking home I thought about Laura and our long and horrible relationship. We didn't have any of the same interests and I always thought she was dumb—we never got along. It was too bad, since I didn't have a sister. It bothered me that I had a cousin who lived near me who was almost my age and that I never got anything out of it. Also, at times I was jealous of her. Aunt Helen and Uncle Jerry didn't have more money than us, but Laura was an only child and they treated her like a little princess. My parents never had that attitude about me and when it came to money they had to think about my darling brother's expenses, not just mine, so to me Laura had always seemed like a spoiled brat.

I knew Mom was going to be amazed when she heard I went to see her voluntarily, and she would really flip out about me helping Laura with her homework.

※ ※ ※

Dad brought home the newspaper as usual. I read it before I went to bed—didn't really want to, but it was on my mind since last night. A girl's body had been found in the woods near route 83 out by Hawthorne. The story said she had been raped and killed somewhere else and her body was dumped there. She had been missing for four days, but there had been no trace of her until yesterday. A man was walking his dog near the woods early in the morning and found her.

※ ※ ※

Had to see the guidance counselor, Mr. Siri. All the seniors were getting appointments to see him. He was pretty nice—he remembered Rob right away and we talked about him. I told him Rob was doing fine. He asked me about my plans, if I had decided what schools I was going to apply to, what field I was interested in, and so forth. He kept looking at my file, which was open on his desk. He said my marks were pretty good, especially second semester last year, and if I kept it up I ought to get accepted as long as I didn't apply to Harvard. I told him I was thinking of applying to one of the top schools even if I couldn't get in and then some others where it was a sure thing or at least a good chance. He didn't say anything. Also I told him how I was trying to get a scholarship, since Robby was in college too and my parents would have both of us to worry about next year. I didn't say anything to him about screwing up this marking period.

He asked me what field I wanted to go into. I told him I wasn't sure, although Mother and Dad would be overjoyed if I became a teacher. Sometimes I thought I'd like to be one (the good kind), but I didn't know if I was cut out for it or if I could control a classroom. Not the kind we had in our school anyway. (Didn't tell him that.) He told me I should do as well as possible on my SAT's. Good advice. He said I could make another appointment to see him if I had any questions—he said I shouldn't put off sending in the applications.

I decided to talk to Clara about it. My parents didn't know much about colleges, and Rob was too busy. Clara had a lot of catalogs, and she'd gone to see two schools near Boston during the summer with her parents. Maybe we could apply to the same schools—we might even be roommates, if she would want to be. I wondered what Rita was going to do, if she still wanted to be a biologist like she once said. She hadn't said anything about it since. I'd like to be a fly on the wall during her appointment with Siri.

❋ ❋ ❋

Rita said something funny the other day—she said she didn't remember anything in her life before the age of nine. Is it because she was so miserable then or what? I can remember things from four or five—a few things. I thought everyone could. She knows all the things she learned at a young age—her abc's naturally, how to read, how to add, probably nursery rhymes, but she can't remember doing anything for the first

96

time. She can't remember any of the teachers before Miss Carroll in fourth grade. I wonder what it's like to have amnesia—to completely forget about major things in your life, like where you live, or to wake up one morning and not know who you are. She said she doesn't feel like all the different pieces of her life fit together.

Saw John lunchtime. We're definitely going to a movie Saturday—we're going to double with Rita and Sam. He's going to get the car.

❊ ❊ ❊

Stupid—I forgot all about calling the clinic. I suddenly remembered it in gym class of all places, then after school I had to get away from everybody so I could make the call before I got home. I went to the drugstore so I could use the phone booth there. It was crowded but I didn't see anyone I knew. I had the card in my wallet—I gave the lady who answered the long number on it and told her I was supposed to call Thursday. She said to wait a minute—I sweated it out until she came back. They had the results. The tests were both negative, but she said the doctor had made a note on my card which said I had to come back and have another blood test in six weeks.

Felt great.

❊ ❊ ❊

Went to the movies, really had a good time with Johnny. We went to the drive-in off route 83—two horror movies. It was strange doubling with Rita, my old childhood friend from the days when we never thought about going with boys. She looked nice—she was wearing a dress and shawl she had made from beautiful plaid material. The movies weren't too great—they didn't take a lot of concentration you might say. Mostly we talked and kidded around and ate.

We turned off the soundbox in the car at times. Rita told another story about her days on the road, this time in Pennsylvania. She said she caught chicken pox from a kid from "Philly" and had to recover in a youth shelter in Harrisburg. She was quarantined there. She made a phone call to her parents to tell them she was alive but didn't intend to ever come home again. Pennsylvania was close to home and it sounded plausible, but Sam said something to her about her vivid imagination—maybe he understands her, or thinks he does, or maybe she tells him more than me. Maybe she's confessed to him that she doesn't always stick to the facts. Sam said when he gets out of school in June he's going up to Nova Scotia and build an A-frame and live there, farm and do carpentry. I always thought a life like that would be great, but then I thought I'd miss the things I was used to—movies, cars, everything. As I was thinking that a bloody head came clumping down the stairs in the movie—struck me funny. Sam had read *Walden* by Thoreau—a man who went to live by himself away from civilization. He was put in jail for not paying his taxes. He wouldn't pay because he didn't believe in the fugitive slave law—returning slaves to the south when they escaped to the north. Sam was a very serious person—in fact he would have been considered odd by most of the kids in my school. I couldn't help thinking he would be perfect for Clara (because they were both serious) although he and Rita seemed to get along. They really did meet at the library. He said something about it. Funny, Rita didn't really know what he was like then. It could have been the same thing that happened to me. He was nice when you got to know him, but he seemed a little "different" at first. There were so many ways of being "different." How could you tell?

After the movies we went to Ronny Kasabach's. I didn't know John knew him that well. There were a lot of kids from school there that I had seen around. I knew their names, but I didn't know them. They had beer and just about everything else. I had a couple of beers and so did John and we talked awhile, then went outside to his car. He started kissing me in the car. For a minute I felt funny, like I was suffocating, then it went away and I was okay. I was a little high from the beer. It helped—I felt safe and out of it. I didn't want to say anything or act weird—didn't really like it though. I didn't want to stay out there with him—I could tell he wanted to. I was going to say something, but then some kids came out and it was a good excuse—he had to move the car away from the driveway. He said he liked me. I guess I do him—can't really tell.

I was a little worried how I'd feel about that—guess it'll be okay.

❀ ❀ ❀

Didn't feel too good Sunday. Had a lot of homework but couldn't get down to it. Dad was out with Mr. Palmer looking at some property in Freevale. I helped Mother with dinner. She made "roast porc a la grandmere." She got the recipe watching Julia Child. I guess she's trying to cook a little better. She asked me about last night. I said we had a good time. I told her about one of the movies and made her laugh. I had that "outsider" feeling with her while we were talking.

Dinner was fine. Dad was in a pretty good mood. He said he had a nibble on the house near Amityville. He might sell it after all. He said business was terrible. I got a sinking feeling when he said it—I always did when he talked that way. I told them about seeing Mr. Siri. I said I was going to try to get a scholarship. He said it would help if I could. I didn't say anything else about college. I felt too discouraged.

There was nothing in the paper about the girl they found in the woods. I looked in Saturday's too—nothing.

I took a bath and got into my pajamas early. I was going to stay up in my room and study, but I couldn't concentrate on anything. I felt confused—didn't know what to do. Finally about nine-thirty I got dressed again. Mom and Dad were in the living room watching tv. I said I had to get some notebook paper at Minnow's and I'd be right back. They didn't think anything of it.

I went down to Schofly's on Elm Street. It was empty except for a couple of people, no one I knew. There were some kids by the magazine rack looking at comics and two older women by the counter. I went to the phone booth back by the prescriptions and called the number I had seen on the train.

A woman answered the phone. She said, "Officer so and so, Police Sex Crimes Analysis Unit." I said I had read in the newspaper about the dead girl they found out by Hawthorne and something had happened to me not far from there, I wanted to report it and give a description of the person. She asked me what happened to me. I told her and gave her a good description of him and of the car. She asked if I had gotten medical care afterwards. I told her I had. She asked if it was at a hospital. I said it was a family doctor and he didn't report it to the police or put it on the records.

She asked, "Would you be willing to come in and file a complaint?" She said I could talk to her or another policewoman. I told her I couldn't, and that there was probably no connection with what happened in Hawthorne anyway. I only wanted to give the description. She said they couldn't use information they got over the phone from someone who called and didn't give her name. If I came in and made a complaint they could use the description and anything I told them. They could give me pictures to look at and if I made an identification they could use that, which was much better than a verbal description. She said the man might have a record so there might be a police file on him or a picture.

I was getting nervous. I told her I couldn't get into it like that. I told her I was sixteen and still lived at home with my parents and went to school, my parents didn't know anything about it and they couldn't live with something like this. I told her I didn't think it would do any good anyway, because there was no connection. She said even if there was no connection with the girl in Hawthorne there might be a connection to other cases, and even if there weren't it should be reported. She said she understood how I felt, but if no one reported it a man like this could attack other women again and again and nothing would ever be done. She said again if I came in I could talk to her, we could set a time and she'd be there. I didn't know what to do. I felt like dropping the phone and running. I said I'd have to think about it and call her back. I didn't give her my name. She told me hers, Mary Duryea. She spelled it.

❀ ❀ ❀

John was out of school. I was glad, I didn't feel like seeing him. Ron Kasabach said hello to me lunchtime. I sat with Rita in her corner in the cafeteria. We didn't talk much about Saturday night. She had her nose in a book and I had my chemistry to do for sixth period.

We had volleyball in gym and I was terrible, got hit in the head with the ball. I didn't see it coming. Felt like a jerk. Sonia started giggling as I picked myself up. We were supposed to be on the same team. Miss Elias told me not to go to sleep during the game. I said, "How about skipping the advice and calling an ambulance?"—trying to make a joke of it as I dusted myself off. She laughed. Sonia said, "Jenny wants an ambulance to pick her up." Pick-up. No one got it but me.

I was talking with Clara after homeroom by her locker. She's so nice, especially compared to a witch like Sonia. I thought of telling her everything and asking her advice. Would that be crazy?

❀ ❀ ❀

I've been thinking about it, and I don't think there's any reason for me to call the police again. I'm sure there's no connection between what happened to me and that thing in the newspaper. Even if there was I don't have any information they could use. I'd get dragged into it for nothing and they wouldn't find him anyway. The policewoman was trying to talk me into it—make me feel guilty. She's probably tough, about ten times more than me, thinks everyone is like her, doesn't know how it is for people like me and doesn't care.

They've probably solved that other thing by now. I haven't been reading the papers.

School was fine. I kept my mind on what was going on in class for once, but in study hall eighth period I started thinking about Grandma and suddenly felt like seeing her. I went straight over from school. She looked like she was glad to see me although the first thing she said was, "What are you doing here?" She looked nice, more cheerful, wearing a black skirt and a print blouse. She wanted me to have some marsala with her to celebrate Rob and Barbara. She seems to think they're formally engaged. I guess that's what they told her since she wouldn't understand the informal way they're going about it.

She started talking about somebody's troubles. I couldn't follow it at first because she was talking in Italian, very rapidly. I thought it was about Aunt Helen and Laura, then I heard "hospital," "in a coma," "divorce." I knew it wasn't that bad over there and I didn't know what she was talking about. I finally realized she was talking about a soap opera she watches every day. I felt like laughing at first, then I felt depressed. I hated to think of her as out of it. I never thought she was and yet when she talked like that it gave me a strange feeling. It seemed like everyone else thought it even though they didn't say anything. Aunt Helen never asked her to help her even though Grandma gets around fine. She was always good to me, better than Mother sometimes, and I used to feel very safe and peaceful in her house, but sometimes it seemed like I was older than her and I had to help her understand things, not vice versa.

I said, "Don't worry about the people on *The Guiding Light*, Grandma. It's only a story."

She said, "Don't worry. It'll turn out all right."

❀ ❀ ❀

When I got home Dad was backing the car out of the driveway. He asked me if I wanted to go with him to see the "white elephant" he'd been talking about. He was meeting a potential buyer there. I got into the car. We drove about two blocks and he asked me if I'd been drinking. He smelled it. I told him Grandma gave me a glass of wine because she wanted to have a toast to Robby. He looked like he didn't think too much of the idea, but he didn't want to criticize her. He drove out on 83 and then he took a couple of turnoffs past the Five Oaks shopping center and onto a road I had never been on before. It was much more rural than I expected. We passed some garden farms, farmers selling fruit and vegetables and cider along the road. There were still pumpkins, too.

The "white elephant" was a strange sight. It must have belonged to a rich family once; it was huge and it had a big plot of land around it too, but now it wasn't kept up. The grass in the yard was so high it looked like a wheatfield. There weren't any trees or shrubbery around the house so it looked bare even with the tall grass around it waving in the wind. The paint was peeling off the shingles. Dad said, "I told Barney—all it needs is a tail and a trunk."

He had the keys. We went inside and I looked all around, upstairs and all over. There were six bedrooms upstairs and three big rooms downstairs. The kitchen was enormous, with an old-fashioned stove. Dad said a couple wanted to buy the house but they needed it for a special use. They had a child who was brain damaged and they had taken two other children, also brain damaged, as foster children. They wanted to take in more if they had the room—it would be half like a family, half like a special school. Dad said the trouble was that the zoning law didn't permit institutional use of the houses in the area, but he was going to try to get a special ruling since the kids wouldn't be going to the public school and wouldn't be a burden on the taxpayers. Looking around the house, even though it was so gloomy and bare and dusty, you could see how great it would be for something like that. Dad said he had thought he wouldn't have a chance with the zoning board because he wasn't in with the politicians, but he had talked to Rob and Barbara about it and they had encouraged him so he was going to try. It was the first I had heard about it.

The couple arrived while I was in the kitchen looking at the stove. They were driving a pick-up truck. Their name was Demaris. They had one of their kids with them, a girl about nine. They had seen the house before. They started talking business with Dad. He told them they had to get different papers for him to submit to the board.

You could tell they wanted to do everything they could to get the house. They looked as old as Mother or Dad, but acted younger. Mr. Demaris came out to the kitchen and started talking about the renovations he wanted to make. He said he could do carpentry and he was going to do all the work himself. He reminded me of Sam. They wanted to put in another bathroom upstairs, and make the dining room into a classroom. Mrs. Demaris was a schoolteacher, and she was going to do most of the teaching. They also wanted to fix up the field outside and turn part of it into a vegetable garden which the kids could work in. They would eat in the kitchen; it was big enough.

The little girl seemed normal at first, just shy and quiet. She had blond hair and wore it in pigtails. She stayed by her father. Mrs. Demaris told me that the kids could learn, but they needed people who understood them and didn't get impatient and treat them like dumbbells. She said they couldn't hide their emotions. For instance, if her daughter talked about something sad that happened to her, or even a fairy tale, she might suddenly start crying from thinking about it. In a regular school some of the kids would make fun of her and she wouldn't be able to stop it. She was also too trusting. If someone in a store saw her with a twenty dollar bill and told her a loaf of bread cost twenty dollars, she would just give them the money—she wouldn't realize someone was trying to cheat her. The other kids were like that too. Mrs. Demaris said they wanted to help the kids grow up so they would be self-sufficient and could live in the world on their own. She started almost pouring

106

her heart out to me. Maybe she thought I could influence Dad. She said when their child was a baby and they saw she wasn't developing normally she and her husband thought it was the end of the world and wondered why it had to happen to them, but now her life had a meaning it didn't have before. I guess she's an idealist. They're from Pennsylvania.

Finally the Demarises settled all their business with Dad and he told them he was going to go to the zoning board and request a ruling. It was dark when we started back. Dad said Mom probably wouldn't make dinner since he hadn't told her where he'd be or when he'd be home. I took up for Mom. We stopped at Kentucky Fried Chicken and ate in the car. Dad was in a good mood about the deal. He said he hoped it would go through. He liked Mr. Demaris. He said the little girl talked to him, and he didn't see how kids like that could survive except in a special place like the Demarises wanted to set up. I told him what Mrs. Demaris had said about getting them ready for the world. He didn't say anything. I think he was thinking it was impossible.

I told him I was thinking about being a teacher and sometimes I even thought about going into the real estate business like him—what did he think? He said I had a long time to decide. Don't think he was really thinking about it too much. It wasn't a good time to talk to him, because he had the zoning board problem on his mind.

Don't know.

Okay day at school. Afterwards, Laura came over with her algebra homework. I helped her the best I could. She was acting nicer. I was watching her while she tried to do one of the problems, bent over the kitchen table. She sticks her tongue at the side of her mouth when she's trying to concentrate. I suddenly got the feeling she was much younger than me.

I'm thinking about telling Mother.

Went over to Eddie Farrell's house Thursday night. I called Lenny's first to see if he was working but he wasn't so I figured he'd be home and he was. He answered the door. I told him I'd been at my grandmother's and I wanted to let him know I had talked to Barini and got the job so we'd be working together again next summer. Eddie said great, but he didn't ask me in so I told him I wanted to talk to him for a minute. Then he did—he told me to excuse the mess in the house.

It wasn't that messy, but it looked different. I hadn't been in his house since his mother died. She used to let me come in for glasses of water when I played with the kids in Grandma's neighborhood. The whole atmosphere in the house was different now, like two bachelors or college boys lived there. There was a model ship on the dining room table, half done, with empty tubes of glue, and pieces of string and wood all over. His father used to be in the navy.

We went into the kitchen.

I said, "A lot of kids are making remarks about me getting picked up. Why did you have to spread it around the whole school?"

He said he didn't.

I said, "Well, somebody did and you're the only one who saw me take the ride with that guy."

He said he might have said something to somebody at Clara's party. I wonder who "somebody" was— probably Sonia's brother. He said he was sorry—he said, "It just seemed funny because no one would think of you doing it."

I told him it wasn't funny to me. I think he was surprised how upset I was. He said he only meant to kid John Fenton since he saw us together at the party.

I said, "If you want to kid him try to think of something else. This is a joke on me, not him."

He said okay. He was embarrassed because it made him look like a gossip, which he was. He said he wouldn't say anything about it anymore. Of course it was already too late—I didn't say that.

It was strange being in Eddie's house talking about it, even though he didn't know. I told him I wasn't going with the guy, I had just taken a lift home from him since it was cold out that night, and I hadn't seen him since. I knew he went to college in Morrisville, but I didn't even know his name. I asked Eddie if he came into Lenny's a lot.

Eddie said he hadn't seen him since the time I was

there, but before that he had come in a couple of times. He was always alone and he usually sat at the counter. I asked about the blue Chevy. Eddie knew a lot about cars and probably noticed them more than I did. He said he'd seen it in the parking lot another time beside the night we drove off. He knew the year and said it had a Connecticut license plate. I acted like it didn't matter that much to me. He probably thought I wanted to meet the guy again or why would I ask.

We started talking about last summer and some of the kids, what a good time we had. He said Barini was going to open up a "garden" in the back with tables and so on in the summer. Sally's going to run it.

After a while I said I had to get home. I felt sorry leaving him in that empty house with the dishes still to do. He was a nice kid, but he had a big mouth.

Friday night Mother and Dad went into New York with the Palmers to see a play. I didn't have anywhere to go or anything to do except homework. I called Clara and asked her if she wanted to come over. She said she couldn't, they were having a "family night" over there. She and her brother were going to play music—he has a little beginner's violin and she plays the piano. Her father was going to build a fire and roast chestnuts. She asked me if I wanted to come over. She said there would be only one piece of music, not a whole evening, in case I was worried about that. I wasn't in a mood to see the happy Andersons because I knew I'd feel out of it, so

I told her I couldn't make it. I did some homework up in my room and then came down and turned on the tv. An old Alfred Hitchcock movie, *Stagefright*, was on and I watched it. It was over at eleven.

I finally decided to go over to Minnow's. It was still open. I wasn't sure until I saw the sign on outside. Someone was in the phone booth so I had to wait. Finally he left and I went in and closed the door and dialed the number. A woman answered, but it wasn't Mary Duryea. I asked for her and waited. It took a few minutes, and then she came on. I told her I had called before. She remembered me. I told her I had found out some other things—I told her about the car, the year, and about the Connecticut license plate. She asked if I knew the license number, but of course I didn't. She asked if I was all right—guess I sounded strange. She said if I wanted to talk to someone, not the police, she could tell me a place to call. I thought she meant a psychiatrist, but she said it was a group of women I could go talk things over with—counseling. They wouldn't contact the police. I told her I was all right. I only wanted to give her information about the car. I knew she was going to start in on how I should come in. I told her I knew I was probably a joke to them down there, calling and not giving my name, and calling back again and not giving my name again. She said they didn't joke about the calls they got. I just suddenly hung up. Didn't want to talk to her anymore.

Mom and Dad got in late, about three. I was still awake. I think Mom was loaded. She was singing something I never heard, probably from the show. They were both laughing.

She looked in my room. I saw the light on the floor even though she was quiet by then. I pretended to be asleep.

I thought of telling Clara or even her parents, but saying it had happened to a friend of mine who wanted advice, but it would be too obvious—they'd know it was me.

❀ ❀ ❀

I went over to Rita's Saturday. She didn't seem too glad to see me. She said she'd been studying. We went up to her room. I told her everything I had been thinking and asked her what she thought I should do. I told her she was the only person who knew all about it and the only one I could ask.

She didn't seem to think it was that important and she wasn't too interested in my phone calls. She seemed to have her mind on something else. She said, "Yeah, well, why don't you do what they want?"— meaning the police, as if it wasn't a big thing.

I said, "This could get me in a lot of trouble."

She said, "With who? Him?"

I said my parents to start with.

She said, "Oh, yeah. Well then you'd better forget about it."

"What do you really think?"

"You better forget about it."

"But you said the opposite just before."

"Look—do what you feel like."

I asked her what she'd do. She said she'd report it. "Why?"

"Because I don't give a damn what anyone thinks. But *you*. . . ."

She had a package of Gauloises, a very expensive kind of French cigarette that she said didn't cause cancer.

She said, "They only cause bankruptcy. They're about fifty cents a shot—each one."

She had taken them from her mother. She gave me one, but no match. I wasn't even thinking about it. I just sat there holding it in my hand unlit. She started talking about different things, nothing to do with what I said. Very casually she dropped in the fact that she had had an experience like mine once. Not really like mine, but she had met a guy in a bus terminal and let him buy her coffee and something to eat and then later she was with him and she ended up doing more than she intended to. She'd never said anything about that before. I was surprised she worked it into the conversation so casually. She said it didn't bother her.

I tried to get back on the subject of what I should do, but she wouldn't let me. She said, "Maybe you're making too much of this whole thing. After all, it was only a screw."

She started talking about something else and I said I had to go. I left and started walking home by Vail Street. I was sorry I had gone over. She practically called me a coward, constantly afraid of what my parents and other people would say. Then the next minute she said I was uptight to even be thinking about it.

I passed Fulton School. It looked completely deserted. No lights on in the whole building. There were Thanksgiving pictures in the black kindergarten windows. The whole place looked haunted—it made me shiver looking at it. I wondered if Mrs. Rinter was

113

dead. She was pretty old when she had our class. She was a wonderful piano player. The pictures looked like the same ones she had us drawing—turkeys, sheaves of wheat, cornucopias. I felt funny thinking about my kindergarten teacher with a Gauloise in my pocket. In a way Rita had contradicted herself all over the place. She said she'd report it if she were me, but then when something like it happened to her she didn't tell anyone, even a friend. (If it was true.) I had been hoping she'd be serious and I could talk to her. When was I going to learn? I couldn't talk to her about anything. I was going to describe the outsider feeling to her, not being part of the world but just watching it. But she wouldn't sympathize with me for feeling out of it because she always felt that way. She was used to it. What a person I chose to confide in.

I couldn't sleep and I went into Mother's room about midnight. Dad was out at his card game and I knew he wouldn't be in till late.

She was in bed reading. She looked surprised when she saw me—she said she thought I was asleep.

I said I had to talk to her. She said sure, what about? I said it was very important, I didn't know what to do, and she had to promise not to tell Dad. She looked worried, she asked me again what it was.

I said I was all right now, but something had happened that I had been too afraid to tell her about when it happened. I was trying to tell her in a way that wouldn't get her too upset, but I couldn't tell her part of it without telling the whole thing.

I told her how it happened. I told her about Iverson

and going to the clinic for tests, and how scared I was until I found out I wasn't going to have a baby. I explained that that was why I was out of school those days and acting upset and rotten to her. I told her about Eddie and the kids at school joking about me being a pick-up and how bad it made me feel even though they didn't know anything. I told her how I had called the police, but now I didn't know what to do.

She listened to it without saying anything. She kept looking at the quilt on the bed. I didn't know what she was thinking. I tried to think of it like two adults talking to each other.

Finally she said, "You should have told me right away. Why didn't you?"

I told her I felt too ashamed. I felt bad about not trusting her, but I couldn't tell her. I just wanted to forget it.

I knew exactly what their room looked like but it was almost like I seeing it for the first time. I could hardly believe I was there and I had really told her. It made it seem more real, not some strange thing in my mind. Everything seemed close.

She didn't yell or get mad. I could tell she was upset but she looked like she felt sorry for me. I started crying with relief. She put her arms around me and told me not to worry. I was so relieved she didn't get mad and blame everything on me. Things started pouring out that I hadn't thought about before. It must have been because she was my mother—I felt safer, like nothing could hurt me because I wasn't alone. I told her all the things that kept streaming into my mind.

She said I should try to go to sleep, and not to worry anymore. She asked me if I was sure I wasn't pregnant. I said I was sure, everything I told her was the truth. It was getting late—I was afraid Daddy would be getting home. I went back to my room—felt relieved, more real, sleepy.

❀ ❀ ❀

I told her the idea I had that my body didn't belong to me anymore. That he was attached to it and it was his, not mine. That I was the only person who ever did anything like it and I didn't fit in with other people anymore. That it must be a punishment for something I did or why would it have happened to me, not Clara, or Rita, or any other girl, but me. I told her I hated myself and I got fits of rage where I wanted to destroy everyone, even her, I hated the world and wanted everyone to be like me, screwed up, filthy, stupid. I hated to see anyone happy. I wanted everyone to know how I felt, to feel the same way. That I wished I had killed him instead of letting him do it, and I hated myself, trembling with fear, doing whatever he said. I told her how he laughed at me. How everything had been getting better, I was forgetting it, and then it started coming up again—I heard that thing on the news, and read it in the newspaper. That the policewoman wanted me to come in but I didn't want to—I wanted to have a normal life and not be different from everybody else.

I told her how things came back to me when I didn't expect it—in a car I suddenly looked at the dashboard, or I might be somewhere and see someone who looked like him or had clothes like his. It would come into my mind again—it would be like vomiting in my mind. I hated it, but I couldn't stop it. I'd think about it again. I'd remember little things—there was a newspaper on the floor in the car, in back; the window was smudged and the streetlight came through it, so dirty. All the little details came back, the way he looked at me, his shirt, the windshield wipers, the slip-covers. I told her I felt filthy, sometimes felt like tearing my skin off, that I threw the clothes away but it didn't make any difference. I told her the feeling I had that I didn't want to feel any part of me he touched. I told her I thought he had turned me into a coward.

I heard her crying in her room. I had gotten up to get a glass of water and heard her through the door. Dad still wasn't home. I didn't know what to do. I just stood there in the hall with a sinking feeling listening to her. I guess she had held all her feelings back with me. I had forgotten that I had had a long time to get used to it and she was hearing it for the first time so it was a shock. I thought I should go in and do something, but I didn't know what I could do, then I felt mad that she was acting like it was such a tragedy. I was sorry I had told her. She didn't know what to do either. Finally I went in. I tried to make her stop crying. I kept saying, "I'm sorry, I'm sorry," and I was.

She's mad at me. I could tell as soon as I saw her this morning, even though she didn't say anything. I

117

guess she had a bad night and started thinking it was my fault. She looked tired. She gave a little sigh before she said anything, as if she was trying to keep her patience. It made me feel like two cents.

She said, "Jenny, I want to ask you one thing. Have you told me the truth about this?"

I said I had.

She said it was hard for her to believe it happened the way I said. She couldn't see how I could have taken a ride from a stranger after all the times she and Daddy had warned me about it.

I said, "Why would I make it up?"

She said she'd been awake all night thinking about it, she hadn't slept at all. Daddy didn't know anything, but she was going to have to tell him.

I said she couldn't, she had promised me. She said she had to anyway. He was upstairs sleeping still. I was afraid he might come down while we were talking. I couldn't face him if he knew. All the time I had been thinking I was terrible not to trust her, but I was right.

I said, "If you tell him I'm not staying here. I'll leave."

I didn't have any place in mind to go, but I said it like I really meant it. Usually she wouldn't have believed me, but she knew I'd been seeing Rita lately so it must have made her think twice.

She said she'd think about it, but she had to do what she thought was right. He was my father. She was talking calmly but I felt like electric sparks were going wildly through my head. I couldn't stand him getting into it. I didn't know how I could have been stupid enough to tell her.

Finally she went to work, looking all upset and tense. I didn't know what to do. I was dressed and ready for school but I didn't want to go. I felt like everything had suddenly gone all wrong and out of my control, just because I had to break down and tell her. I couldn't stand going through the long day at school, but I didn't want to stay in the house—didn't feel safe.

I left the house soon after Mother, but I didn't go to school. I walked over to Edgewood, just to go somewhere, and then kept going to the highway and the shopping mall. No one stopped me to ask why I wasn't in school. There were a lot of people and everybody was busy. I walked around and went into Gimbel's and Sam Goody's and looked around. I decided to go to Grandma's. I headed for home about noon—I was pretty sure Dad would be gone. When I got there I ran upstairs and started throwing some things into my overnight bag—my school books and some clothes, knee socks, underwear, and so forth. I was just grabbing anything. All the time I felt like I was suddenly going to look around and see Mother or Dad. I was out of the house in about ten minutes. I forgot my toothbrush and a lot of things but I was too nervous to go back. I headed over to Grandma's. I didn't see anybody as I walked there with my suitcase.

I told her I was going to stay with her for a while if it was okay—I'd sleep on the sofa. I said my room was being painted and I couldn't stay there until it dried and everything was moved back. I would never have had the nerve to lie like that before, but I couldn't think what else to say. It was stupid because

119

Rob's room was empty, but she seemed to accept it. She asked why I wasn't in school. It was about one o'clock. I said we only had a half day because of some special tests. She seemed to believe it. She trusted me, or maybe she didn't want to think about anything being wrong.

She made me some lunch and I ate with her out in the kitchen. We watched a quiz show and *The Guiding Light*. After it was over she started talking about Grandpa, acting like his death was quite recent. I ate a whole plate of cookies out of nervousness.

About three-thirty I went into her bedroom where she couldn't hear me and called Mother at work. I didn't say I didn't go to school. I told her where I was and said I wasn't coming home until she promised not to tell Dad.

Right away she asked, "Did you tell her?"—very accusingly.

I told her what I had said. She was relieved—she said, "Don't say a word to her about this. It would kill her."

Mother was keeping her voice down. I could tell there were people there and she couldn't talk freely. I could hear some kids in the background.

I told her again that I wasn't coming home unless she promised not to tell Dad. I felt safe because I knew they wouldn't come over to the house and make a scene in front of Grandma. Mother said she was going to talk to him tonight, she had thought it over and there was nothing else she could do. She said she knew he'd be upset and it was just as well if I stayed where I was tonight.

It was useless talking to her. I told her again she'd promised not to tell him. I said she had let me down.

She said, "You let me down too."

❋ ❋ ❋

I had to go out and buy a toothbrush, but otherwise I had everything I needed except pajamas. Grandma gave me one of her flannel nightgowns to wear. She went to bed early and I made a bed on the sofa and turned out the lights. I didn't go to sleep. I had too much to think about—what was going on at home. I thought maybe, possibly, Mother had changed her mind and not told him.

The streetlight was coming in through the front windows so I could see all around the room. It was like having a nightlight—I didn't pull down the shades. It was strange sleeping on the sofa in Grandma's old-fashioned house, with the carved furniture all around me, two lion's faces in the endtables and a cupid over the mirror. They were all in shadows but I could see them. She had an old clock that gave a little chime every hour on the hour—the last one I heard was at two o'clock—I must have been asleep by three.

❋ ❋ ❋

I went to school from Grandma's. I knew if I stayed out I'd just worry all day and get more nervous. I was tired from not sleeping too well, but no one noticed anything. I didn't tell anyone what happened. I would have told Rita but I was really mad at her.

After school I went to the library and stayed there an hour or so, then went back to Grandma's. When I got there Mother was in the kitchen. She had stayed out of work. She and Grandma were sitting around the table talking, and I could tell Mother hadn't told her anything. She didn't act mad—she just said she had come by so we could go home together.

I didn't want to make a scene and I didn't want him coming over and dragging me home so I went.

When we got outside she said, "Daddy and I had a long talk last night."

"Does that mean you told him?"

She said, "Yes. He was very upset, but he wants to talk to you."

"About what?"

"About what happened."

"I don't want to talk about it. It's none of his business anyway."

She said, "It *is* his business. He's your father."

I didn't know what was going on. Did it mean he was sorry it happened or was he mad at me?

She wasn't acting nasty, but I could tell she was going to take his side, whatever it was. She said he had a right to feel the way he did, any father would feel that way about his daughter. She said I had to make my peace with him—I couldn't keep avoiding him forever.

❀ ❀ ❀

Dad didn't get home until six and I had to sweat it out for nearly two hours. Finally I heard the car in the driveway. I went down to the living room. He was in his chair—he gave me a stern look when I came in, but at least it looked like he had his temper under control. It was probably good I wasn't home when he heard about it the first time.

122

He said, "All right. Sit down."

I sat down.

He said, "I want to hear the truth about this."

I said I had told Mother everything.

He said he didn't think I was telling the whole story.

I asked, "What do you think happened?"

He said, "I want to hear it from you."

I said I'd already told Mother, and I was sure she told him all about it last night, I didn't want to go through it all again. I was trying not to show how scared I was. I felt like my heart was knocking against my ribcage and they could hear. I could hardly look at him.

He said, "You don't seem to realize how serious this is."

I said I did.

He said he and Mother had worked hard all their lives to bring me up right and give me a decent home and all they had asked was that they could be proud of me and that I wouldn't disgrace them. His face was getting red. I had never seen him so upset, or mad.

I said, "I'm sorry, Daddy."

He said, "Who is this person?"

I said I didn't know him, like I had told Mother. He said I should be ashamed of myself, there was no excuse for getting into a stranger's car. He asked if it was true I'd been going around telling people.

I said, "I had to go to a doctor."

He said, "Your mother said you've gone to the police with this story."

He was acting like it was a trial and he was the judge. The way he said "this story" made me start trembling with rage. All this time Mother was just sitting on the sidelines watching.

I said, "What are you? The jury?"

She just looked at me—she didn't know what I meant. Dad said I'd better watch my mouth. He asked me again who I'd told. He made it sound like I was going around spreading the story, as if I'd want to. He said he was going to get the truth out of me. He said I'd disgraced myself and him and the whole family.

I said I wasn't staying. I couldn't listen to that anymore. I got up and started out of the room. I was going back to Grandma's. He said to stop but I didn't. He came after me and grabbed me before I could get out the front door. I jerked my arm away but I couldn't get loose. He said again I should be ashamed, looking at me like he hated me. I told him to let me go but he wouldn't. I called him a rotten bastard and he slapped me. I hit him back. He didn't expect it—he stopped like he didn't know what to do, but he wouldn't let go. I felt desperate to get out of the house and away from him. I started screaming at him. I said I knew he didn't love me, all he could think of was himself and he never stopped to think about me. I said it was stupid of him acting like I was so bad to him and the family—they didn't know anything about it or have to go through anything except hearing about it—it was me. I said I didn't give a damn if he didn't believe me and I didn't care what he thought about me. I kept calling him stupid. I could hear Mother saying, "She's hysterical, she's hysterical," trying to calm him down. He gave me a real slap—I probably would have crashed against the wall if he hadn't been holding my arm. He probably thought it was going to bring me back to my senses but it was just the opposite. I hit him back. Every time he hit me I hit him back and called him a bastard or stupid. I didn't want to let him scare me and break down so I'd just give up and start crying and saying he was right. I felt like I was going to get killed but I couldn't stop. I told him he was just as bad as Iverson, he didn't know anything and he didn't care. If I had been killed he'd be sorry, but since I survived he treated me like dirt as if everything that happened was my idea. He didn't know anything about what I went through. I said I didn't care what he thought of me—I hated him. He looked like he was taking a pause before he was going to kill me. Mother kept saying, "Leave her alone, Bob, she's hysterical." She said it over and over.

With Mother in there I broke away from him and ran out of the house, ran back to Grandma's in the dark. They didn't try to stop me.

❀ ❀ ❀

I couldn't hide how upset I was to her so I said I'd had a fight with Dad and I had to stay with her again. I said they knew and it was okay with them. She didn't ask me what it was about. She looked worried—she said I should do what my father said and not get him mad. She said, "Who takes care of you?"

She told me to get anything I wanted to eat. She watched television. The phone rang and I got it. It was Mother. All she said was, "I thought you'd be there. Are you all right?"

I said I was staying. She didn't argue or have much to say. I hung up and sat with Grandma. We didn't talk about it. Before she went to bed she said, "It'll be all right tomorrow."

I couldn't believe I was still alive.

❀ ❀ ❀

Grandma was talking in her sleep—I guess because she was upset. I had to get up and close the door to her bedroom. I was exhausted. I slept a little, but then I woke up and couldn't stop worrying. The streetlight was shining in through the windows again and everything was shadowy. The clock chimed—four o'clock.

I tried not to think about Dad. I didn't know what I was going to do or even where I was going to live. I lay huddling on the couch with the blanket around me like a cocoon. I thought about Rob. I wondered if they'd called him. I wondered what he'd say. I thought about calling him—he might be up all night studying. Maybe he'd be understanding and take my side and help me, but maybe not.

I turned on the radio very low to get my mind on something else. I got an all-night show where people phoned in and talked on the air. I had never heard it before because I was never listening to the radio at that hour. People called and talked about things in the news, and then there was a man who said he had seen a flying saucer over in Flushing Meadow Park. The announcer started tearing into him. He said, "Have you recently escaped from anywhere? How did you manage to get out of your strait jacket and pick up the phone? Was it difficult or did you have help?" The man kept saying, "I'm telling you the truth, Ed. So help me God." I felt sorry for anyone who would call that show for sympathy. I knew how the man felt—all alone, trying to get through to someone—but even I didn't believe him. It seemed hopeless.

I dozed off and had a bad dream. I was wandering around in a strange city—Detroit—where I've never been. I didn't know anyone there and I didn't have any money. Cartoon characters were walking around the streets, people and animals—lions, too. I had a transistor radio in my pocket. I kept playing it. I was thinking, should I sell it or keep it for company? I came to a department store and looked in the window. It was a furnished room, just like I needed. The next thing I knew I was suddenly inside the store looking out at the street at all the people and animals through the thick glass. Then it started to crack. Cracks were growing all through the window glass, branching out in every direction. I suddenly woke up. I felt panicked, like something terrible was going to happen. I sat up on the sofa. Everything was okay, the room was the same, the furniture, even the lion faces in the wood. The radio was still on, very low—a commercial for Wonder Bread.

❀ ❀ ❀

I have a black eye. I discovered it this morning in the mirror while I was getting ready for school. Decided not to go.

I stayed in the house with Grandma. We talked and watched television in the kitchen. Later I went into her bedroom and closed the door and tried to work on my history. I told her I bumped into a door last night. She gave me an icebag to put on it.

In the afternoon I put some make-up on my eye and went out to the library and sat around in the reading room a while. I was dying to get out of the house. The weather was cold but beautiful.

Neither Mom nor Dad called tonight.

❋ ❋ ❋

Went back to school. I thought I had disguised my black eye with make-up, but as soon as I arrived someone said, "What happened to you?" I said I'd had an accident, I fell and bumped into something. Rita was out of school. John was sitting with some other kids lunchtime—he didn't come over to my table and I wasn't about to go over there. Maybe he didn't see me. Didn't see Sonia.

❋ ❋ ❋

I called Mary Duryea tonight. I told her I'd decided to come in and talk to them, but when I gave her my address she told me I wasn't in their jurisdiction. She didn't know where I lived when I called before. She said I should go to the police here. She checked and told me what I should do. Even though it wasn't her business I started telling her all my troubles at home and started crying on the phone. She said she was sorry, and maybe I should change my mind about calling a group for counseling. She talked to me awhile and tried to comfort me, but what could she do.

❀ ❀ ❀

I reported it Saturday. I called the number Mary Duryea gave me and asked to speak to a policewoman. There was only one in the town, but I got to see her. Her name was Officer Carrier. She had a little office with a partition. I had never seen the inside of the police station before. It reminded me of the Post Office. There were a couple of cops hanging around the desk drinking coffee and laughing about something. Thank God I didn't have to talk to them.

It didn't take too long. She asked me questions and filled out a form. It was the same one the police used for everything, with spaces for car theft, make and model, and so on. I gave my address at home, not at Grandma's. She was quite businesslike. She asked if I had gotten medical attention and I told her about Dr. Iverson. She said she was surprised my parents had never warned me about taking rides with strangers, but except for that she didn't lecture me. I had the feeling she thought I was stupid to take the ride and she would never have done it, but at least she was experienced with the law and she knew I wasn't the one who broke it. She asked me about my eye. She thought I got it from him. I told her I got it at home. She didn't say anything, but I could tell she felt sorry for me because after that she acted friendlier, not so businesslike.

She asked me why I took so long to report it. I said I didn't know what to do at first. I asked what they were going to do. She said they would ask questions at Lenny's and other places, especially about the car, and they would check files on the car. They would also check with other police departments. I might have to come back later and look at pictures. I told her about Eddie, that he had seen him and the car.

She said it was too bad I hadn't come to them right after it happened, before I got cleaned up and washed away all the evidence. Now it would just be my word against his, but if he was in trouble for other offenses it would be different. I asked her if she knew anything about the dead girl found in Hawthorne. She said the police hadn't found anything as far as she knew.

She said I was the second person who had reported a rape in the last year. The other one was a girl younger than me. She came with her mother. She said they were both more upset than me. She said most people didn't report it. Sometimes someone would be arrested and he would confess to a lot of other crimes and none of them would have been reported. She asked me why I came in. I said I didn't know and it was true.

❀   ❀   ❀

Before I went to sleep, in the dark room, I thought about him trying to get even with me if he found out I told. He probably never thought I would. He seemed to despise me for being weak but he'd hate me more now. I guess he wouldn't laugh anymore. Wonder if he ever thought of it afterwards. Wonder what made him that way.

❀ ❀ ❀

Rita came over to Grandma's Sunday. She said
she'd been by my house and Mother told her where I
was. She wanted to borrow my history book; she was
out of school Friday. I wasn't too glad to see her. I
told her I didn't like some of the things she said last
time I saw her. She didn't even remember what she
had said.

She and Grandma hadn't seen each other since Rita
was about ten so they talked for a little while, then
Grandma went out to the kitchen. Rita lit up a
Gauloise and sank back into the sofa. I told her about
all my troubles at home, but they were the last thing
she could sympathize with. She thought it was hilari-
ous that I had hit Daddy. She didn't realize how terrible I felt when he talked to me like that, or how
strange I felt not living at home anymore. She said,
"At least your grandmother doesn't live in Missouri."
She was surprised I had gone to the police. She said
she didn't think I was going to. I said she didn't understand all the troubles I had—at home, kids finding
out at school, at Lenny's, and everywhere. Also if
anyone at school found out it would fit in with the
"pick-up" joke and made me look bad. I never knew
when I was going to run into someone who was going
to unexpectedly give me a hard time. She said what's
the difference. She said, "Don't you ever hear a little
voice in your head saying it's time to get a bus
ticket?" She didn't understand me—she seemed to
think I was hopeless—but I didn't understand her either, how she could be the way she was, so calmly
trying to blow smoke circles in the air. She made it

seem like you could forget your whole life completely and go somewhere else, as if there were somewhere else.

I always thought Grandma was lonely and would love to have me around as much as possible, but it gets her nervous having her routine upset. She gave me a look while we were eating in the kitchen. It reminded me of a movie I saw called *The Man Who Came to Dinner*—about a man who came to someone's house for dinner and stayed for years. I think that's the way Grandma feels about me at times. Last night she said, "When are you going to get it settled?"

My eye is much better.

Mother called when I got back from school. She said I had to come back. I said, "Why? So he can murder me?" She said I shouldn't talk that way. I said I wouldn't go back until he promised not to lay a hand on me. She said he had calmed down, he didn't want to talk about it anymore, he was going to try to forget it ever happened. She said she hoped I'd apologize to him. It was incredible the way she took his side, but I should have expected it. I said if he left me alone I wouldn't make any trouble—didn't say anything about apologizing. Didn't tell her I was wearing out my welcome at Grandma's. I knew I had to go back sometime.

❀ ❀ ❀

Went home tonight—brought the suitcase and everything. Saw Dad in the living room as I was going up to my room. Too bad my eye was all healed. I could have tried to make them feel guilty for a change instead of vice versa. Dad just said hello to me and I said hello back—that was all.

Happy to be back in my room again and sleep in my own bed.

❀ ❀ ❀

Report cards. I really loused up this marking period. Corry failed me.

❀ ❀ ❀

Friday night Mom and Dad went out with the Palmers. I was home. About eight o'clock the phone rang. It was Mrs. Demaris, the woman who wanted to buy the white elephant. She wanted to talk to Dad. I told her he wasn't home. She said she wanted to leave a message, that he should get in touch with them if anything else came on the market and she wanted to thank him for trying. The zoning thing hadn't worked out—I didn't know. She didn't sound too discouraged—she said they were going to keep looking.

I went up to my room and stayed there all night—homework and playing music. The phone rang again pretty late. It was Sally, calling from Lenny's. She said she wanted to let me know someone had been there asking questions. At first Mr. Barini thought it was about his license for the annex and went crazy, but then they found out it wasn't that, it was about me. Sally said she thought I should know so I could straighten it out. She thought it was a mistake. The cop spoke to Eddie, Barini, and Dolores, the other waitress, and Dolores told Sally. The cop didn't mention my name, just asked about a customer who had picked up a girl, but before I talked to him Eddie had said something about it at work too so everyone connected it with me right away. I said it wasn't a mistake, I really did have trouble with a guy I met there and I reported it. Sally said she was sorry. She was trying to be nice. She said she missed seeing me and I should come in and have a talk with her. I said I would. I felt bad after I hung up. I figured if she heard about it a lot of other people would too.

I finally had a talk with Mom and Dad. I was going to tell Mother first, but then I decided it would be better to say it while Dad was there too and get it over with. I told them I had reported it to the police and I wanted them to know in case anyone called the house for anything. Dad said I should have talked to him first. I don't know what he would have told me to do. He said it was a bad thing to get mixed up in. I could tell he didn't want another fight and he knew it was too late anyway since I'd already done it. I told them that Officer Carrier, the policewoman, said it happened to other people besides me and that I had done the right thing to report it. I said I wasn't the one who broke the law and the police knew it. They didn't say anything. I don't know what they were thinking. I asked them if they had told Robby. They hadn't.

They weren't yelling or anything. They were both acting okay to me, but different. Dad was taking the attitude that I was mentally deranged when we had our fight and I didn't understand what I was saying and didn't mean it. It wasn't true. I did mean it, but I wasn't about to start another argument with him and risk getting killed. He didn't think he ever acted crazy. I don't think I was ever crazy or even borderline, although that "outsider" feeling was quite strange. Don't have it anymore.

❀ ❀ ❀

Monday. School was okay. Nobody said anything.

Johnny didn't talk to me lunchtime. I know he saw me. He was sitting with some kids at the table by the gym door when I came in. Maybe he didn't like the way I acted when we doubled with Rita and Sam, or maybe he heard something and didn't want people to see him with me, thinking he'd be in for some kidding. Maybe just my imagination.

135

❀ ❀ ❀

When I got home Laura called. She had come by during the week, and no one was home. She didn't know I was at Grandma's. Wonder what Mother would have said if she had been home. I was happy to hear Laura's voice—it seemed like I hadn't talked to her in years. She sounded happy—all excited about Thanksgiving. She's going to the game with a senior and she was all excited about that. We're doing algebra tomorrow over her house.

Mother left a note in the kitchen saying I should get groceries because she had to stay late at Grinnell's and wasn't going to have the time. She left a list and some money. I put on my coat again and went to the A & P. I decided to make dinner—I knew how to make chicken and I thought things would go a little better if I did. She wanted me to get chicken and vegetables and something for dessert—we didn't have much in the house.

I got the stuff and I was walking back along Edgewood when Bob Cris, Sonia's brother, and a bunch of guys drove by—Ronny K. and some others. There were five guys in the car. The windows were open and I could hear them down the block. They saw me and stopped and asked if I wanted a ride home. I was glad to see them—I was surprised they stopped. I wasn't in with that crowd and I was wondering if Johnny was cutting me because of that or what. I was getting into the back with my bag of groceries when Kasabach made some remark about me always being glad to take a ride. He was laughing looking at me and I was smiling back, then I realized what he meant. It was the way he said it and the way he looked at me. They were all laughing. I didn't know what to say because it wasn't out in the open. I said I remembered I had to go back to the store for something, I wasn't going home so I didn't need the ride.

He said, "Hey, how come you changed your mind?"

I said, "You don't have any right to joke about that."

He acted surprised and said, "What are you talking about?" But he was laughing.

I shut the door and started walking. I knew I was going to start crying and I didn't want them to see me.

Felt miserable. Wished I'd gone by Vail Street—I wouldn't have run into them.

❋ ❋ ❋

Dinner was fine. Mom and Dad liked the chicken. Things seemed more like they were before.

❋ ❋ ❋

I began to think maybe I was imagining the whole thing with Ronny and Bob Cris. I wished it was that, but I didn't think so. Why would he say it and why would they be laughing like that?

❋ ❋ ❋

Someone told Clara. She didn't tell me who. It was in school today. She called tonight—she didn't believe it at first. (My friend.) I told her it was true. We talked for a long time. Mother and Dad were watching television so I didn't have to worry about them hearing. I told Clara I thought maybe it was getting around school. It wasn't the police who gave my name, it was Eddie before. I could tell Clara felt sorry for me and was pretty shocked. She would never have taken the chance like I did so she almost didn't know what to say. I could tell she didn't think it could ever have happened to her. She thought I should go to Mr. Wiley's office with my parents and ask him for a chance to make up my grades, she said it was the same as if I was sick all last marking period. That was the way she always was, practical. I told her I didn't know if I could make it up anyway. She wanted to meet me before school tomorrow. I was glad—I felt like when I got up in the morning I'd think about meeting her instead of just going to school alone.

Didn't feel too good before I went to bed. I kept thinking about that rotten Kasabach. I thought of telling Mother or even Dad, but I was afraid they wouldn't sympathize, just say I told you so. I thought of calling Robby but then I thought it wasn't a good idea—I didn't know. I was nervous about going to school. No one could do anything to me, but I dreaded the idea of someone like Kasabach making a remark in front of a lot of people—they didn't know what it was like.

Mom and Dad went to bed about eleven-thirty. I was lying in bed worrying and thinking till late. I started crying thinking about Kasabach and Cris, then I started thinking about other people in school—I didn't know how they'd act. I was wondering if Eddie was going to say anything to me. Finally about two o'clock I began to calm down. Running into those guys had got me upset, but then I started to get over it. I thought about meeting Clara at school, and Laura after, and I thought of going to Lenny's maybe after school Wednesday and talking to Sally—she wanted to see me and she knew all about it. I thought I shouldn't think all the time about what the stupidest people said. I decided to hang around with Clara or even Rita the first day and probably it wouldn't be so bad, and if someone like Bob Cris or Sonia said anything I could just tell them to go to hell.

"Why Me? The Story of Jenny" is fiction, but it refers to several organizations that are real.

Many new programs to combat rape and to help rape victims have been established since 1970. They are an outgrowth of the women's movement. Anyone wishing to learn about anti-rape groups in her locality can write or phone The Rape Crisis Center, P.O. Box 21005, Washington, D.C., zip 20009, phone (202) 333-7273, or contact the local National Organization for Women (NOW) office listed in the telephone directory.

There are public health clinics for the detection and treatment of venereal disease in most major cities and in many smaller communities as well. Minors are treated at these clinics without parental consent.

I would like to express my thanks to the women in The New York City Police Department, The Rape Study Group, New York Women Against Rape, and The New York City Department of Health whom I consulted while writing the book.

The Sex Crimes Analysis Unit of The New York City Police Department has a special telephone number, 233-3000, which has been set up to receive calls reporting rape. The number is always answered by a policewoman. New York Women Against Rape is a group formed by women to help rape victims; it holds meetings where they can come together and talk over the practical and emotional problems they face. The New York City Department of Health operates V.D. clinics throughout the city. There are similar groups and programs in other parts of the country.

The Rape Study Group, funded by The Police Foundation, conducted a study in 1974, working with The New York City Police Department, for the purpose of developing better police procedures for handling rape cases and then making their findings available to other police departments in The United States. The women in this group provided me with information based on their analyses of cases reported in New York City during that year.

P.D.